THE WHY AND HOW OF AUDITING

© 2019 Charles Hall. All rights reserved. No portion of this book may be reproduced, stored in a retrieval system, or transmitted in any form or by any means—electronic, mechanical, photocopy, recording, scanning, or other—without permission of the author.

While every precaution has been taken in the preparation of this book, the author assumes no responsibility for errors or omissions, or for damages resulting from the use of the information contained herein.

Interior book layout by Caley Hindman

ISBN-13: 978-0-578-51973-9
ISBN-10: 0578519739

PRAISE FOR
The Why and How of Auditing

———

Need a quick-reference audit guide? This is it. Charles walks you from the beginning of the audit process all the way to the end, an excellent plain-english guide.

Mark Wiseman, CPA, CMA, Partner
Brown, Edwards & Company, L.L.P.
Roanoke, Virginia

This is a great how-to, hands-on guide that will help you conduct a quality audit and provide value to your clients. Go over a chapter a week with your audit team. The book provides the why and how behind your audit programs and workpapers.

James H. Bennett, CPA, Managing Member
Bennett & Associates, CPAs PLLC
Ann Arbor, Michigan

Thanks Charles for clarifying what's important in an audit. Recommended reading for any auditor level.

Jay Miyaki, CPA, Partner
Jay Miyaki, LLC
Honolulu, Hawaii

The author steps through each audit area in a simple manner and clearly explains topics that are often complex by providing numerous examples and personal anecdotes. I highly recommended this text to anyone in the financial statement audit profession.

Jacob Gatlin, CPA, PhD
CDPA, PC
Athens, Alabama

Charles Hall's "The Why and How of Auditing" is comprehensive, yet easy to implement. This guide will enhance the effectiveness of your audit engagements.

Armando Balbin, CPA, Partner
Downey, California

I highly recommended Charles Hall's latest book, "The Why and How of Auditing." Charles takes a complicated subject and makes it simple. Our team found it particularly useful in the areas of questions to ask, procedures to follow, and work paper examples.

Bill Burke, CPA, Partner
Burke, Worsham and Harrell, LLC
Bainbridge, Georgia

A must-read for auditors! The Why and How of Auditing is insightful, practical, and rich with ideas. Charles takes a complex topic and breaks it down into an easy to read, well-defined road map.

Kathryn Fletcher, CPA, MBA, Partner
Draffin Tucker
Atlanta, Georgia

The Why and How of Auditing
TABLE OF CONTENTS

PREFACE

Each year, Vince Lombardi (the revered coach of the Green Bay Packers) held a pigskin up and said, "This is a football." And he did so before the best players in the world. Why? He knew that winning is all about basics: blocking, tackling, passing, running. Understanding fundamentals brings clarity and power. And that's what I'm after in the *The Why and How of Auditing*.

The Pain of Not Understanding Auditing

Recently, I received this email:

> Charles,
>
> Our peer review is now complete. The reviewer hammered our planning and risk assessment documentation. Now we have to take remedial auditing classes. It's embarrassing. We thought we were doing a good job, but apparently not.
>
> The other issue was "a lack of documentation." Then, strangely, he said we sometimes do *too much* work. Too little, too much—not sure how to find the right balance.
>
> Can you help?
>
> Tom

Moving from Wasteful Auditing to Efficient Auditing

This book is all about striking the right balance. We're not after a fat file or a flat file. We're after a just-right file. One that supports our opinion without extraneous information.

Lucy used to say to Charlie Brown, "I will hold the ball, and you kick," but as Charlie Brown would lean into his launch, she would pull away. And you remember the result: Charlie Brown, lying on his back.

Some audit procedures, like the invitation to kick, are tempting. They call us like a familiar friend, but they are a waste even if we have done them for years. In the end, they leave us staring at the sky.

We need to know what is *best* and what is *necessary*. When you're done with this book, you will know what you need to do.

The Organization of This Book

This book addresses three key audit areas.

1. Planning.
The first four chapters of this book are about planning. This section includes client acceptance, risk assessment, auditing for fraud, and creating your audit plan.

2. Performing.
Next, in chapters five through twelve, we look at performing the audit. You'll find specific account balance guidance for areas such as cash, receivables, payables, and debt.

3. Completing.
And finally, chapter thirteen teaches you how to complete your audits.

My Perspective

I have audited companies, nonprofits, governments, and other entities in the United States for the last thirty-four years. The guidance in this book is based mainly on my knowledge of generally accepted auditing standards (in the United States) and upon my experience in using those standards. It's from that perspective that I write.

This publication is not an exhaustive audit guide. (If that is what you are after, this is not your book.) Rather, this book is designed to make auditing understandable. It's concise on purpose.

Sample Audit Guidance

While there is no one standard audit methodology, I provide audit guidance in relation to typical account balances. For example, in the *The Why and How of Auditing Cash* chapter, I discuss common relevant assertions such as existence and cutoff. However, every company and every audit is different. The relevant assertions, the risk of material misstatements, and the audit procedures vary from entity to entity. Why? Because every entity is different. Therefore, you'll want to consider how this book applies to your particular audits.

Let's Begin

It is my sincere desire that you enjoy this book and that you find yourself reaching for it often.

I want *you* to be the best auditor possible.

So let's begin.

To my twin brother, Harry. Thankful for his constant encouragement.

PART ONE
Planning the Audit

CHAPTER 1
The Why and How of Acceptance and Continuance

───────

Client acceptance and continuance may be the most important step in an audit, but it's one that gets little attention. A prospective client calls saying, "Will you audit my company?" and we respond, "sure." While new business *can* be a good thing, we need to evaluate the relationship. Not doing so can lead to significant problems.

New Relationships

My daughter recently met a young man on Instagram. Not unusual these days. Now the relationship is entering into its third month. They talk every day for two or three hours. So far, they have not been in the same room and not even in the same state. Skype, yes. In the presence of each other, no. That's happening at the end of this month. (He lives ten hours away.)

What do Mom and Dad think about all of this? Well, it's fine. My wife checked him out on Facebook (I know you've never done this). And my daughter has told us all about her "fella" and his family. We like what we're hearing. He has a similar family background and beliefs. He has a job (yay!) and a college degree.

Why do we want to know all the details about the young man? Because relationships matter. My wife and I want what is best for our daughter. Why? Because we want her to be happy.

Client Acceptance

And that's what good relationships create: happiness. The same is true with clients. As Steven Covey said, "think win, win." When the customer wins and your CPA firm wins, everyone succeeds and mutual needs are met.

Careless CPAs accept business with only one criteria: the ability to pay.

While getting paid is important, other factors are also critical.

Here are a few:

- Is the potential client ethical?
- Are you independent?
- Do you have the technical ability to serve them?
- Do you have the capacity to serve them?

Are They Ethical?

I want my daughter to marry a guy with beliefs that correspond with who she is. Is he honest? Would he steal? Is he transparent? Who are his associates? What do others think of him?

We ask similar questions in accepting a new client. Audit standards require us to consider whether the prospective client has integrity. If the company is not morally straight, then there's no need to move forward—regardless of the audit fee.

Are You Independent?

The time to determine your firm's independence is the beginning, not at the conclusion of the audit. As a peer reviewer, I can tell you that firms don't always fully vet their independence. Consider what happens during a peer review when a firm is not independent, and it has issued an audit opinion. The original audit report will be recalled, and I'll bet the company asks for and receives a full refund of the audit fee. And there's that impact on the peer review report.

Pay attention to nonattest services such as preparation of financial statements. If the client has no one with sufficient skill, knowledge, and experience to accept responsibility for such services, you are not independent.

Do You Have the Technical Ability to Serve Them?

If you can pick up a client in an industry in which you have no experience, should you? Possibly, but it depends on whether you can gain an understanding of the client and their industry. Some new customers are not complicated. With those, you can move forward. But with others, it may be better to pass on the opportunity. Or maybe you can partner with another firm that has the requisite knowledge and experience.

Do You Have the Capacity to Serve Them?

A prospective client calls saying, "Can you audit my company? We have a December 31 year-end, and we need the audit report by March 31." After some discussion, I think the fee will be around $75,000. But my employees are already working sixty hours a week. Should I take the engagement?

My answer is no unless I can create the capacity. How? I can hire additional personnel, or maybe I can contract with another firm to assist. If I can't create the capacity, then I'll let the opportunity go.

Far too many firms accept work without sufficient capacity. When this happens, corners are cut and firm members suffer. Stuffing even more work into busiest time of the year is not the wise thing to do. You'll lose people, and if the engagement is deficient, peer review results will suffer.

When you don't have the capacity to accept new clients, consider whether you should discontinue service to some existing customers (those who are difficult to work with or who don't pay).

The Continuance Decision

Quality control standards call for continuance protocols. I previously said some CPAs don't give proper attention to acceptance. So, how about continuance? Even worse. It's as though we think there's a permanent relationship.

Each year, we should ask, "Would I accept this client now?" If the answer is no, then why do we continue to serve them?

Here are a few questions to ponder:

- Has the client paid their prior year fees?
- Am I still independent?
- Does the client demand more time than the fee merits?
- Do I enjoy working with the client?
- Is the client's financial condition creating additional risk?
- Is the client acting in an ethical manner?

Each year, well before the audit starts, ask yourself these questions. And then consider, "Is the bottom 5% of my book of business keeping me from accepting better clients?" My experience has been that when I have the capacity, new business appears. But when the capacity is lacking, I don't. The decision to hold on to bad clients is a decision to close the door to new ones. Don't be afraid to let go.

Risk Assessment Starts Now

When should you start thinking about risk assessment? Now.

Whether you are going through the initial acceptance procedures or you are making your continuance decision, think about risk now. Assuming you accept the client, you'll be a step ahead as you begin your audit. Ask questions of the potential client such as:

- How is your cash flow?
- Do you have any debt with covenants?
- Who receives the financial statements?

- Has the company experienced any fraud losses?
- How experienced is management?
- Why are you changing auditors?

Retain this acceptance documentation and use it in your audit planning after you become the auditor. That way, you're not asking the same questions a second time.

Acceptance and Continuance - A Simple Summary

- Acceptance and continuance may be the most important audit step
- Don't accept unethical clients
- Independence is necessary for acceptance of and continuance with an audit client
- Ask yourself if you have the technical ability to perform the audit
- In accepting and continuing to serve an audit client, consider your capacity (how busy are you when the audit is to be performed?)
- Conditions change from year to year, so make your continuance decision early (you may have been independent last year, but not this year)
- Risk assessment should start in the acceptance phase of the audit

CHAPTER 2
The Why and How of Risk Assessment

Are auditors leaving money on the table by avoiding risk assessment? Does risk assessment lead to better peer review results? In this chapter, you'll see that understanding risk assessment is a key to greater profit and positive peer review results.

Audit Risk Assessment as a Friend

Audit risk assessment can be our best friend, particularly if you desire efficiency, effectiveness, and profit—and who doesn't? Risk assessment tells you what to do—and what to omit. In other words, risk assessment is the doorway to maximum impact with minimal effort.

Why do some auditors avoid audit risk assessment?

- We don't understand it
- We are creatures of habit

Too often auditors keep doing the same as last year (commonly referred to as SALY), no matter what.

But what if SALY is faulty or inefficient?

Working Backward

The old maxim "Plan your work, work your plan" is true in audits. Audits—according to professional standards—should flow as follows:

1. Determine the risks of material misstatement
2. Develop a plan to address those risks
3. Perform substantive procedures
4. Issue an opinion

Some auditors sometimes go directly to step three and use the prior year audit programs to satisfy step two. Later, before the opinion is issued, the documentation for step one is created "because we have to." In other words, they work backwards, because they don't *really* plan.

Is there a better way?

A Better Way

Audit standards call us to do the following steps:

1. Understand the entity and its environment
2. Understand the transaction level controls
3. Use planning analytics to identify risks of material misstatement
4. Perform fraud risk analysis
5. Assess the risks of material misstatement (identify where risk exists)

While we might not complete these steps in this order, we do need to first perform our risk assessment and *then* assess risk.

Okay, so what risk assessment procedures should we use?

Audit Risk Assessment Procedures

AU-C 315.06 states:

The risk assessment procedures should include the following:

1. Inquiries of management, appropriate individuals within the internal audit function (if such function exists), others within the entity who, in the auditor's professional judgment, may

have information that is likely to assist in identifying risks of material misstatement due to fraud or error
2. Analytical procedures
3. Observation and inspection

I like to think of risk assessment procedures as detective tools used to sift through information and identify clues. Just as a good detective uses fingerprints, lab results, and photographs to paint a picture, we use walkthroughs, planning analytics, fraud inquiries, and the understanding of the entity to create a risk portrait.

Understand the Entity and Its Environment

The audit standards require that you understand the entity and its environment.

You might start by asking management this question, "If you had a magic wand that you could wave over the business and remove one problem, what would it be?" The answer tells you a great deal about the entity's risk.

You want to know what the owners and management *think* and *feel*. Every business leader worries about something. And understanding fear illuminates risk. Think of risks as threats to objectives. Your client's fear tells you what the objectives are—and the threats.

To understand the entity and its threats, ask questions such as:

- How is the industry faring?
- Are there any new competitive pressures or opportunities?
- Have key vendor relationships changed?
- Can the company obtain necessary knowledge or products?
- How strong is the company's cash flow?
- Has the company met its debt obligations?
- Is the company increasing in market share?
- Who are the key employees and why?

- What is the company's strategy?
- Are there any related party transactions?

Once you know your client's risks, relate them to the risks of material misstatement. After all, the audit opinion is in relation to whether material misstatements are present.

As with all risks, we respond based on severity. The higher the risk, the greater the response.

We'll respond to the risks of material misstatement at two levels: financial statement and transaction.

Responses to the risk of material misstatement at the financial statement level are general, such as appointing more experienced staff for complex engagements. Responses to risk of material misstatement at the transaction level are more specific such as a search for unrecorded liabilities. But before we determine responses, we must first understand the entity's controls.

Understand the Transaction Level Controls

We must do more than just understand transaction flows (e.g., receipts are deposited in a particular bank account). We need to understand the related controls (e.g., who enters the receipt in the general ledger, who reviews the receipting activity, etc.).

As we perform walkthroughs or other risk assessment procedures, we gain an understanding of the transaction cycle, but, more importantly, we gain an understanding of controls. Why? To see if controls are properly designed and implemented.

The use of walkthroughs is probably the best way to understand internal controls. As you perform your walkthroughs, ask questions such as:

- Who signs checks?

- Who has access to checks
  (or who has electronic payment ability)?
- Who approves payments?
- Who initiates purchases?
- Who can open and close bank accounts?
- Who posts payments?
- What software is used? Does it provide an adequate audit trail? Is the data protected? Are passwords used?
- Who receives and opens bank statements? Does anyone have online access? Are cleared checks reviewed for appropriateness?
- Who reconciles the bank statement? How quickly? Does a second person review the bank reconciliation?
- Who creates expense reports and who reviews them?
- Who creates the monthly financial statements? Who receives them?

As we perform walkthroughs, we ask the payables clerk (for example) certain questions. And, as we do, we make observations about the segregation of duties. Additionally, we inspect documents such as purchase orders.

This combination of inquiries, observations, and inspections allows us to determine if a risk of material misstatement is present. A weak control is a risk indicator.

As you perform your walkthroughs, gain an understanding of the entity's information technology and related controls.

Information Technology Risks

Depending on the size and complexity of the business, information technology can be simple or quite elaborate. Regardless, gain an understanding of the application and general computing controls.

When you perform your accounts payable walkthrough, for example, review application controls. Some systems make payments based on purchase orders. Others pay when the purchase order, the receiving document, and the invoice agree (commonly known as a three-way match).

Additionally, review the entity's general information technology controls. Ask questions such as:

- Are passwords required to access each software component (e.g., accounts payable)?
- Who has the ability to make changes to the company's software? What is the process for testing and tracking software changes?
- How are technology changes documented? Who does this?
- What are the physical security requirements for computer and network systems?
- Is cloud-based technology used? If yes, how?
- Is software access limited to persons that must have permission? Is access assigned so that proper segregation of duties is ensured? Who provides access to software and when? Is access discontinued upon an employee's termination?
- What are the backup procedures? Who is responsible for this duty? Has recovery been tested? If yes, when?
- Does the entity use antivirus software? If yes, what and how is it updated? How often? Who is responsible for this duty?
- Are firewalls in use? If intrusions occur, who is notified? Who is responsible for protection of the company's information? Have the entity's personnel been trained with regard to phishing and malicious emails?
- Are periodic technology reports provided to management and those charged with governance?
- Does the company have written technology policies? Who monitors those?
- Have there been any significant technology problems?
- What is the educational background and experience of the

information technology personnel?

- Does the entity outsource technology duties?

Complex information technology systems may require the auditor to use a specialist.

As you review the information technology system, remember the purpose for gaining this understanding: to see if the application or general controls create a risk of material misstatement.

Another risk identification tool is planning analytics.

Planning Analytics

Planning analytics assist in identifying risks of material misstatement. I like to use multiple-year comparisons of key numbers (at least three years, if possible), and key ratios.

Unexpected variations in numbers can signal that fraud or error is present.

(See Appendix A for a detailed look at preliminary analytics.)

Fraud Risks

In every audit, inquire about the existence of theft. And while performing walkthroughs, look for control weaknesses that might open the door to fraud.

We should also consider management override of controls and intentional overstatements of revenue

Fraud risk is addressed in the next chapter, so, this is all I will say about theft for now.

Sometimes the greater risk is not fraud but errors.

Same Old Errors

Have you ever noticed that some clients make the same mistakes every year? Usually it's your smaller clients—those with poorly trained staff.

One way to identify potential misstatements due to error is to maintain a summary of the larger audit entries made over the last three years. If your client tends to make the same mistakes, you'll know where to look for potential errors.

Now it's time to pull all of the above together.

Creating the Risk Picture

Once you complete the risk assessment procedures, synthesize the disparate pieces of information into a composite image. You are, at this point, bringing the information into one distilled risk snapshot. What are you bringing together? Examples include:

- Control weaknesses
- Unexpected variances in significant numbers
- Entity risk characteristics (e.g., level of competition)
- Large related-party transactions
- Occurrences of theft

And why do you do this? As a basis for your audit strategy and audit plan.

With the risk snapshot in hand, you can now assess risk. How? By using the risk of material misstatement (RMM) formula.

Assess the Risk of Material Misstatement

Understanding the RMM formula is key to identifying high-risk areas.

What is the RMM formula?

Simply put, it is:

Risk of Material Misstatement = Inherent Risk X Control Risk

Using the RMM formula, we are assessing risk at the assertion level. While audit standards don't require a separate assessment of inherent risk and control risk, consider doing so anyway. Why? For a better understanding of risk.

Once we complete our risk assessment process, control risk can be assessed at high—simply as an efficiency decision. Alternatively, you can assess control risk below high and test controls for effectiveness.

The cash risk assessment might appear as follows (if control risk is assessed at high for all assertions):

ASSERTION	INHERENT RISK	CONTROL RISK	RMM
Existence	High	High	High
Completeness	Low	High	Moderate
Accuracy	Moderate	High	Moderate
Rights and Obligations	Low	High	Moderate
Cutoff	Moderate	High	Moderate

The cash risk assessment might appear as follows (if controls related to existence are tested and found to be effective):

ASSERTION	INHERENT RISK	CONTROL RISK	RMM
Existence	High	Moderate	Moderate
Completeness	Low	High	Moderate
Accuracy	Moderate	High	Moderate
Rights and Obligations	Low	High	Moderate
Cutoff	Moderate	High	Moderate

RMM is based on inherent risk and control risk. So, we consider the risk of each component in arriving at RMM as a whole. I commonly use the lower of inherent risk and control risk, but there is no requirement to do so. Other auditors use something other than the lower of the two. For instance, if inherent risk is low and control risk is high, they might assess the RMM at moderate or high. RMM depends on risk. Some high risk assessments are "really high" and others are "somewhat high." Thus, RMM depends on the actual risk for each assertion.

Some auditors use percentages in assessing risk, though I am not a fan of doing so. But if you are mathematically inclined, percentages may work better for you. Personally, I like using categorical values: low, moderate, and high.

(See appendix B for *Understanding the Audit Risk Model.*)

The Inputs and Outputs

Audit planning inputs come from risk assessment procedures such as walkthroughs and planning analytics.

What are the outputs of risk assessment? The audit strategy and the audit plan (audit programs).

In chapter four, I'll show you how to create your audit strategy and audit plan.

Risk Assessment - A Simple Summary

- Risk assessment is your friend
- Determine the risks of material misstatement *prior* to developing your audit plan
- Your risk assessment tools include:
  - Understanding the entity and its environment
  - Walkthroughs
  - Planning analytics
  - Fraud inquiries
- Gain an understanding of the entity

- Understand the internal controls of the business and determine whether they are properly designed and whether they have been implemented
- Use planning analytics to uncover unexpected changes in numbers
- Inquire of management, other employees, and those charged with governance regarding fraud
- Based on the evidence gathered, develop your risk picture (a snapshot of where the financial statements might be misstated)
- The risk of material misstatement = inherent risk X control risk (use this formula to assess the risk of misstatement)
- Develop your audit strategy and audit plan to address identified risks of misstatement

Next we'll take a look at how to perform risk assessment procedures related to fraud.

CHAPTER 3
The Why of How of Auditing for Fraud

What is an auditor's responsibility for fraud in a financial statement audit? In this chapter, I'll answer that question.

Let's take a look at the following:

- Auditor's responsibility for fraud
- Turning a blind eye to fraud
- Signs of auditor disregard for fraud
- Cooking the books
- Theft
- Discovering fraud opportunities
- Inquiries required by generally accepted auditing standards
- The accounting story and big bad wolves
- Documenting control weaknesses
- Brainstorming and planning your responses

Auditor's Responsibility for Fraud

I still hear auditors say, "We are not responsible for fraud." But is that true? The detection of material misstatements, whether caused by error or fraud, is the heart and soul of an audit. So writing off our responsibility for fraud is not an option. We must plan to look for material fraud.

Audits will not, however, detect every material misstatement— even if the audit is properly planned and conducted. Audits are designed to provide *reasonable assurance*, not perfect assurance. Some material frauds will not be detected. Why? First, an auditor's time is limited. He can't audit forever. Second, complex systems can make it extremely difficult to discover fraud. Third, the number of fraud schemes—there are thousands—makes it challenging to consider every single possibility. And, finally, some frauds are so well hidden that auditors won't detect them.

Even so, auditors should not turn a blind eye to fraud.

Turning a Blind Eye to Fraud

Why do auditors not detect fraud?

- We don't look for fraud because we don't understand it
- We disregard the importance of walkthroughs
- We believe that auditing the balance sheet is enough

Think of these reasons as an attitude—a poor one—regarding fraud. This disposition manifests itself in the audit file with signs of disregard for fraud.

Signs of Auditor Disregard for Fraud

A disregard for fraud appears in the following ways:

- Asking just one or two questions about fraud
- Limiting our inquiries to as few people as possible
- Discounting the potential effects of known theft
- A lack of walkthroughs
- No fraud brainstorming sessions
- Vague responses to brainstorming and risk assessment (e.g., "no means for fraud to occur; see standard audit program" or "company employees are ethical; extended procedures are not needed")
- Unchanged audit programs though control weaknesses are noted

In effect, some auditors dismiss the possibility of fraud, relying on a balance sheet approach.

So how can we understand fraud risks and respond to them? First, think about fraud incentives. The reasons for theft vary, depending on the dynamics of the business and the people who work there.

Second, consider the opportunity element of fraud. Fraudsters can enrich themselves indirectly (by cooking the books) or directly (by stealing).

Cooking the Books

Start your fraud risk assessment process by asking, "Are there any incentives to manipulate the financial statements?" For example, does the company provide bonuses or promote employees based on profit? If yes, an employee can *indirectly* steal by playing with the numbers. Think about it. The chief financial officer can inflate profits with just one journal entry. Just debit receivables and credit revenue. How easy is that?

Some companies juice their profits by manipulating estimates. They might, for example, intentionally decrease the allowance for uncollectibles. Why? Doing so increases net income. This is why audit standards require retrospective reviews of certain estimates—to ensure there is no bias.

Auditors should review the prior year estimates and then consider what actually happened. In looking at the prior year allowance for uncollectible (say for December 31, 20X2), the auditor examines the actual bad debt write offs made during 20X3. Doing so assists the auditor in determining whether the prior year estimate was appropriate. Then he reviews the current year estimate for reasonableness.

Some estimates such as a bank's allowance for loan losses are complex. The more complicated the estimate, the easier it is to manipulate. So, use retrospective reviews to assess the reasonableness of estimates.

While cooking the books is a threat, the more common fraud is theft.

Theft

Some employees enrich themselves *directly* through theft. But employees can only steal if they have opportunity. Where does opportunity come from? Weak internal controls. Therefore it's imperative that auditors understand the accounting system and more importantly, related controls.

Discovering Fraud Opportunities

My go-to procedure in gaining an understanding of the accounting system and controls is a walkthrough. Since accounting systems are varied, and there are no "forms" (practice aids) that capture all processes, walkthroughs can be challenging. Therefore, we have to roll up our sleeves and get in the trenches.

For most small businesses, performing a walkthrough is not difficult. Pick a transaction cycle; start at the beginning and follow the transaction to the end. Ask questions and note who does what. And as you do, inspect related documents. Then, ask two questions:

- What can go wrong?
- Can material misstatements occur without detection?

In more complex companies, break the transaction cycle into pieces. You know the old question, "How do you eat an elephant?" And the answer, "One bite at a time." The process for understanding small companies works for a large ones as well. Just break it down and allow more time.

Discovering fraud opportunities requires the use of procedures such as inquiries of personnel, observations of controls, and inspections of documents. Of the three, inquiry is the most common. Auditing standards do not, however, permit the use of inquiry alone. Use a combination of inquiry, observation, and inspection.

Inquiries Required by Generally Accepted Auditing Standards (GAAS)

GAAS requires auditors to inquire of management and others about the occurrence of fraud. We should also ask about any suspected theft or allegations of the same.

Audit standards state that auditors should inquire of management regarding *their* fraud risk assessments. We should ask:

- Who is responsible for assessing the risk of financial statement fraud?
- How often is this risk assessment performed?
- How does the organization monitor the threat of fraud?
- Who receives and reviews the fraud risk assessment and monitoring reports (including management and those charged with governance)?
- How often do they receive these reports?
- How does management communicate its ethical views (e.g., code of conduct)?
- What fraud detection procedures are performed by their internal auditors? How does internal audit address the risk of fraud in their annual audit plan? Do internal audit employeees report directly to those charged with governance rather than to management alone?

If management has no method of detecting fraud, might this be a control weakness? Yes.

In smaller entities, you may get a deer-in-the-headlights look when you ask the above questions. These companies usually have no internal audit staff and may not be aware that they are responsible for fraud prevention. They might even say to you (the auditor), "Isn't that what you do?"

What are the respective roles of management and auditors regarding fraud?

- Management *develops* and *operates* the accounting system
- Auditors *review* the system in order to plan and perform audit procedures to detect material misstatements (including theft)

In short, the company creates the accounting system, and the auditor gains an understanding of it. It is not the external auditor's job to *prevent* fraud. Detect it, yes (at least, if it's material). Prevent it, no.

The Accounting Story and Big Bad Wolves

Think of an accounting system as a story. Your job is to understand the narrative. As you describe the accounting system, you may find missing pieces. And when you do, you ask more questions. Why? To complete the story.

The purpose of writing the narrative is to identify any "big, bad wolves."

Threats in childhood stories are easy to see—wolves are hard to miss. Not so in walkthroughs. It is only in connecting the dots—the workflow and controls—that the wolves materialize. So, how long should the story be? That depends on the size of the organization.

Scale your documentation. If the transaction cycle is simple, the documentation can be short. If the cycle is complex, more details are needed. Regardless, focus on control weaknesses that allow material misstatements.

Documenting Control Weaknesses

I usually summarize internal control strengths and weaknesses within the walkthrough narrative. For example:

Control Weakness: The accounts payable clerk (Judy Jones) can add new vendors and print checks with digital signatures. She can create new vendors and send checks without anyone else's involvement.

Highlighting weaknesses makes them prominent and useful in your brainstorming session.

Brainstorming and Planning Your Responses

Now you are ready to brainstorm about how fraud might occur.

Armed with knowledge of the company, the industry, fraud incentives, and the control weaknesses, you and your audit team are ready to think like a thief. And why would you do this? To unearth how fraud might occur. Once you do, use these ideas to develop responsive audit procedures.

The Auditor's Responsibility for Fraud

I started this chapter by saying I'd answer the question, "What is an auditor's responsibility for fraud?"

Our responsibility is spelled out in the language of the standard audit opinion (the italics are the authors):

> The procedures selected depend on the auditor's judgment, including the *assessment of the risks of material misstatement* of the consolidated financial statements, *whether due to fraud* or error. In making those risk assessments, the auditor considers internal control relevant to the entity's preparation and fair presentation of the consolidated financial statements *in order to design audit procedures* that are appropriate in the circumstances, but not for the purpose of expressing an opinion on the effectiveness of the entity's internal control.

The purpose of fraud risk assessments—in a standard audit

engagement—is to assist the auditor in designing appropriate substantive audit procedures. It is not to opine on internal controls. (Some audit engagements do include opining on internal controls, but most do not.)

Additionally, even well-performed audits will not detect all material fraud. As we saw above, some frauds are extremely difficult to detect. Audits are designed to provide *reasonable assurance*, not perfect assurance. The standard audit opinion states (the italics are the authors):

> Our responsibility is to express an opinion on these financial statements based on our audit. We conducted our audit in accordance with auditing standards generally accepted in the United States of America. Those standards require that we plan and perform the audit to obtain *reasonable assurance* about whether the financial statements are free from *material misstatement.*

In summary, the auditor should conduct the audit in a manner to detect material fraud. But it is possible that some material frauds will not be detected.

Auditing for Fraud - A Simple Summary

- Auditors should design their audits to detect *material* misstatements whether caused by error or fraud
- An auditor's disregard for fraud is evidenced by a lack of fraud-related work paper documentation
- Fraud occurs when (1) the client intentionally misstates financial statement numbers (cooking the books) or (2) assets are stolen (theft)
- Walkthroughs shed light on how fraud might occur
- Auditors should inquire of management and those charged with governance about fraud

- Documenting internal control systems is similar to writing a story (where you point out the big bad wolves—control deficiencies)
- Brainstorm (with your audit team) about how fraud might occur based on your understanding of the entity and its controls
- The purpose of understanding controls in a standard audit is to develop audit procedures, not to opine on controls
- Plan and perform your audit to provide reasonable assurance that the financial statements are free from material misstatement

Next, we'll look at how to develop your audit plan.

CHAPTER 4
The Why and How of Audit Planning

Now it's time to develop your materiality and planning documents.

Audit Materiality, Audit Strategy, and Audit Plan

To be in compliance with audit standards, you need to develop your planning materiality, audit strategy, and audit plan

As you create your materiality, strategy, and plan, remember your ultimate goal: the audit opinion. And what does it say? That the financial statements are fairly stated (if the opinion is unmodified). But how do we know if the financial statements are fairly stated? Materiality.

Planning Materiality

Materiality is a financial reporting concept, but we use it in auditing.

The Financial Accounting Standards Board defines materiality this way:

"The omission or misstatement of an item in a financial report is material if, in light of the surrounding circumstances, the magnitude of the item is such that it is probable that the judgment of a reasonable person relying upon the report would have been changed or influenced by the inclusion or correction of the item."

This definition is not a formula such as one percent of total revenue (or any other computation), but we need clearly defined boundaries, don't we? That's why auditors compute materiality using formulas. Even so, materiality is also qualitative.

Examples of material misstatements include:

- Misstatements of a financial statement line
- The omission of a significant disclosure
- An incomplete disclosure
- An unreasonable estimate

Computed materiality is the level of acceptability for any of the above. But, again, qualitative factors are considered. For example, related party transactions might merit a lower materiality.

Auditors create layers of materiality including:

- Financial statement materiality
- Performance materiality
- Particular account materiality

In computing materiality, what should you consider?

Materiality Considerations

First, consider the common needs of the readers. Readers of financial statements—management, owners, lenders, vendors, and others—make decisions based on the audited information. You should develop materiality in light of their common needs.

Second, consider which benchmark to use. Some examples are total revenues, total assets, or net income. Choose a benchmark that is relevant and stable. Often total assets or total revenues are good choices.

Third, determine appropriate percentages to apply to the benchmark.

Financial Statement Level Materiality

How do you create your financial statement materiality (also called planning materiality)? Usually, you will apply a percent to a benchmark. You might, for example, use one percent of total assets.

But what percentages should you use? Most CPAs defer to third-party publishers that provide materiality forms. Others create their own percentages. Either way, materiality must be reasonable. What is reasonable? The Financial Accounting Standards Board defines materiality as an omission or misstatement "such that it is probable that the judgment of a reasonable person…would have been changed or influenced by the inclusion or correction of the item."

Performance Materiality

Undetected misstatements can adversely affect our consideration of materiality.

What if, for example, your materiality is $100,000? And what if the passed adjustments are $90,000 and undetected misstatements total $50,000? In such a situation, an unmodified audit opinion might *appear* to be correct—even though material misstatements are present. You need a cushion to lessen the risk that uncorrected misstatements and undetected errors exceed materiality. But how? By using performance materiality.

What is performance materiality? It is the use of materiality at a transaction or account or disclosure level (rather than at the financial statement level). For example, performance materiality for cash could be $150,000 and financial statement materiality could be $200,000. In this example, a detected error of $175,000 in cash would not be acceptable.

How does performance materiality differ from financial statement materiality? Performance materiality is applied at a transaction or account or disclosure level. Financial statement materiality applies to the entity as a whole.

Performance materiality calls for thresholds at the account level (e.g., receivables/revenue) and is usually calculated using 50% to 75% of financial statement materiality. Why the range? To provide room for judgment.

If the risk of material misstatement is low, then a higher percent might be merited. If the risk of material misstatements is high, then a lower percent (e.g., 55% of materiality) can be used. Also, if your client is not inclined to record detected misstatements, use a lower percent. You don't want misstatements—in whatever form— to wrongly influence the decisions of financial statement users.

Particular Account Materiality

Additionally, you may use—in some instances—an even lower materiality (that is, lower than your performance materiality). You, for example, might desire greater assurance with regard to an estimate. If you are auditing a bank's allowance for loan losses, you might use 25% of materiality (or an even lower percent). Why use a lower percent? Because this estimate is complex and risky.

Materiality is Iterative

As you perform your audit, revisit your initial materiality computations. Audit adjustments might change the initial benchmark totals. For instance, if audit adjustments increase total assets, then materiality should increase accordingly, assuming total assets is your benchmark.

In addition to materiality, document your audit strategy.

Developing Your Audit Strategy

What should you include in your audit strategy? AU-C 300.08 states that the audit strategy should include:

- The characteristics of the engagement
- The reporting objectives
- The significant factors
- The results of preliminary engagement activities
- Whether knowledge gained on other engagements is relevant

Also, consider what resources you need to perform the engagement. Will you need a specialist? Do you need data mining software? What audit team members do you desire?

The audit strategy is the big picture. Here you document considerations such as:

- The scope (what are the boundaries of the work?)
- The objectives (what are the deliverables?)
- The significant factors (is this a new or complex entity?)
- The risk assessment (what are the risk areas?)
- The planned resources (what team members do you need?)
- The timing (when is the audit due?)

Should the audit strategy be lengthy? Not necessarily. For smaller entities, it can be a short memo. What are we after? A summary of risks, needed resources, and objectives.

An audit strategy could, for example, address the following:
- Deliverables and deadlines
- A time budget
- The audit team
- Key client contacts
- New accounting standards affecting the audit
- Problems encountered in the prior year
- Anticipated challenges in the current year

- Materiality
- Partner directions regarding key risk areas
- References to risk assessment work papers (those that support the strategy)

In addition to the strategy, you need an audit plan, sometimes referred to as the audit program.

Developing Your Audit Plan

The audit plan is the linkage between planning and further audit procedures. What are "further audit procedures"? They are the actions to be taken in response to the risks of material misstatement. These actions include substantive procedures and tests of controls. The audit program links back to the identified risks and points forward to the substantive procedures and test of controls.

Creating the Audit Program

How—in a practical sense—do you create audit programs? Most auditors tailor their prior year audit programs. That works as long as you revise them to address the *current* year risks. Audit programs are not static documents—at least, they should not be. The current year audit programs *can* be the same as last year, as long as the risks are the same. But if risks are different, then change the audit programs accordingly.

Sufficient Audit Steps

How do you know if you have adequate audit program steps? Look at your risks of material misstatement (RMM)—which should be assessed at the assertion level (e.g., completeness). Audit steps should address all high and moderate RMMs in material transaction classes.

Additionally, AU-C 330.18 says the auditor is required to apply substantive procedures to all relevant assertions related to each *material* class of transactions, account balance, and disclosure. So, the audit program should include steps for all material areas, even if risk is assessed at low.

For example, if plant, property, and equipment is material and all related assertions are assessed at low, plan and perform audit procedures for this area. If the existence assertion is relevant (and it usually is), then plan an audit step to address it. You could, for example, vouch invoices supporting additions to property.

If the RMM is high, then the audit plan should include additional steps to address those risks. For example, if there is a risk that fictitious vendors might be added, plan procedures to address that risk.

If the RMM is moderate, you'll perform standard audit procedures for that area. For example, if the existence assertion for cash is moderate, you might plan to test bank reconciliations.

If the RMM is low and the transaction area is not material, then audit procedures can be minimal. After all, your audit opinion addresses material misstatements.

As you build your audit plan, link your risk assessments to your audit programs.

Linking Risk Assessment with the Audit Program

How can you integrate your risk assessment with your audit programs? Linkage, which is the process of connecting risk assessment and responses. On the risk assessment work paper, the auditor might say, "Because the controller can add new vendors and process payments by himself, we will perform a test for fictitious vendors." Then the auditor adds an audit program step to test for this risk. By doing so, the auditor links the risk assessment to the response.

We can also create linkage by putting relevant assertions next to each audit step. Then the RMMs and audit procedures are connected. For example, if your risk assessment for the accounts payable completeness assertion is high, then put a C (for completeness) next to your search for unrecorded liabilities audit program step. Now the risk (the understatement of payables) is linked to the audit step (the search for unrecorded liabilities).

Creating Efficiency in the Audit Plan

In developing your audit program procedures, remember you have two options: substantive procedures and test of controls.

Once you complete your risk assessment work, ask, "Which is more efficient? Testing controls or performing substantive procedures?" Then plan accordingly.

Generally, I assess control risk at high. While auditors can't default to a high control risk assessment, they can—once the risk assessment work is complete—decide to assess control risk at high.

Why do I often assess control risk at high? Because I don't desire to test controls (often involving a sample of forty to sixty items—or more) for effectiveness. Control risk assessments below high must be supported by a test of controls. If controls are not tested, then there is no basis for the lower control risk assessment. But the testing of controls often takes more time than the alternative: substantive procedures.

For example, suppose a company pays two invoices totaling $4.1 million (98% of the total property additions for the year). Is it more efficient to vouch two invoices or test the property controls? More than likely, vouching invoices. In this situation, I elect to assess property control risk at high—that way, I don't have to test the operating effectiveness of the controls.

Nevertheless, this logic—substantive tests take less time than testing controls—is often *less* true for more complex organizations. Larger businesses process more transactions and tend to have better controls. So it *can* be better to test controls for some entities. I also believe that a test of controls for effectiveness is more useful in some transaction areas such receivables, payables, and payroll.

The choice is yours. You can perform substantive procedures or you can test controls—or you can do both. The important thing is to respond to identified risks.

Audit Planning - A Simple Summary

- Materiality is a financial reporting concept used in auditing
- Financial information is material if omitting it or misstating it could influence users' decisions
- Performance materiality is the application of materiality at a transaction level or account balance level such as receivables (and is often 50% to 75% of financial statement materiality)
- An even lower materiality percent can be applied to risky areas (e.g., a bank's allowance for loan losses)
- Document your audit strategy as a summary of objectives, resources, and risks
- Create your audit plan (audit program) based on identified risks
- Audit programs should address all moderate to high risk assessments for each significant audit area
- The auditor is required to apply substantive procedures to all relevant assertions in each *material* class of transactions, account balances, and disclosures (even if all RMMs are low)
- The audit plan can include substantive procedures, test of controls, or a combination of the two

There you have it: the creation of the audit strategy and the audit plan. Your strategy includes the risks, needed resources, and objectives. And your audit programs are responsive to the identified risks. You are good to go. Now it's time to perform your procedures.

In the upcoming chapters, we will look at how to audit:

- Cash
- Accounts receivable and revenues
- Investments
- Property
- Accounts payable and expenses
- Payroll
- Debt
- Equity

PART TWO
Performing the Audit

CHAPTER 5
The Why and How of Auditing Cash

———

Now we shift gears. We move from risk assessment and planning to auditing transaction areas. Cash is a good place to start.

Auditing cash tends to be straightforward. We usually just obtain the bank reconciliations and test them. How? By vouching the outstanding items to the subsequent month's bank statement. Additionally, we send bank confirmations. But are such procedures always adequate? Hardly.

Recall the Parmalat and ZZZZ Best Carpet Cleaning frauds. In those businesses, cash thefts were covered up with fake bank statements and fake bank confirmation responses. Millions were lost and audit firm reputations were sullied.

How to Audit Cash

In this chapter, we will take a look at the following:

- Primary cash assertions
- Cash walkthrough
- Directional risk for cash
- Primary risks for cash
- Common cash control deficiencies
- Risk of material misstatement for cash
- Substantive procedures for cash
- Common cash work papers

Primary Cash Assertions

First, let's look at assertions.

The primary relevant cash assertions include:

- Existence
- Completeness
- Rights
- Accuracy
- Cutoff

Of these assertions, I believe existence, accuracy, and cutoff are most important. The audit client is asserting that the cash balance exists, that it's accurate, and that only transactions within the period are included.

Classification is normally not a relevant assertion. Why? Because cash is almost always a current asset. But when bank overdrafts occur, classification can be in play. Negative cash balances are sometimes shown as liabilities on the balance sheet.

Cash Walkthrough

Second, perform your risk assessment work in light of the potential relevant assertions.

In performing cash walkthroughs, ask questions such as:

- Are timely bank reconciliations performed by competent personnel?
- Are *all* bank accounts reconciled?
- Are the bank reconciliations reviewed by a second person?
- Are all bank accounts on the general ledger?
- Are transactions appropriately cut off at period-end (with no subsequent period transactions appearing in the current year)?
- Is there appropriate segregation between persons handling cash, recording cash, making payments, and reconciling the bank statements?

- What bank accounts were opened in the period?
- What bank accounts were closed in the period?
- Who has the authority to open and close bank accounts?
- Are there any restrictions on the bank accounts?
- What persons are authorized to sign checks?
- What is the nature of each bank account (e.g., payroll bank account)?
- Are there any cash equivalents?
- Were there any held checks (checks processed and signed but not mailed) at period-end?
- Who makes deposits and how? Who records them?

As we ask questions, we also inspect documents (e.g., bank reconciliations) and make observations (e.g., who is doing what?).

If control weaknesses exist, we create audit procedures to address them. If during the walkthrough we review three monthly bank reconciliations and they all have errors, we will perform *more* substantive work to prove the year-end bank reconciliation. We might, for example, vouch *every* outstanding deposit and disbursement.

Directional Risk for Cash

Third, consider the directional risk of cash. What is directional risk? It's the potential bias that a client has regarding an account balance. A client might desire an overstatement of assets and an understatement of liabilities since each makes the balance sheet appear healthier.

The directional risk for cash is that it is overstated. So, perform procedures to ensure that cash is not overstated, such as testing bank reconciliations.

Primary Risks for Cash

Fourth, think about the risks related to cash. Primary risks include:

- Cash is stolen
- Cash is intentionally overstated to cover up theft
- Cash accounts are intentionally omitted from the general ledger
- Cash is misstated due to errors in the bank reconciliation
- Cash is misstated due to improper cutoff

Common Cash Control Deficiencies

Fifth, think about control deficiencies noted during your walkthroughs and other risk assessment work. In smaller entities, it is common to have the following control deficiencies:

- The same person receipts and/or disburses monies, records those transactions in the general ledger, and reconciles the related bank accounts
- The person performing the bank reconciliation does not possess the skill to perform the duty
- Bank reconciliations are not timely performed

Risk of Material Misstatement for Cash

Sixth, using the information you gathered, assess your risks of material misstatement. The assertions that concern me the most are existence, accuracy, and cutoff. So my RMM for these assertions is usually moderate to high.

My response to higher risk assessments is to perform certain substantive procedures: namely, bank confirmations and testing of the bank reconciliations. As RMM increases I examine *more* of the period-end bank reconciliations and *more* of the outstanding reconciling items.

Substantive Procedures for Cash

And finally, it's time to determine your substantive procedures in light of your identified risks.

My customary audit tests are as follows:

- Confirm cash balances
- Vouch reconciling items to the subsequent month's bank statement
- Ask if all bank accounts are included on the general ledger
- Inspect period-end deposits and disbursements for proper cutoff

The auditor should send confirmations directly to the bank. Some individuals create fake bank statements to cover up theft. Those same persons provide false confirmation addresses. Then the confirmation is sent to an individual (the fraudster) rather than the bank. Once received, the fraudster replies to the confirmation as though the bank is doing so. You can lessen the chance of fraudulent confirmations by using Confirmation.com, a company that specializes in bank confirmations. Alternatively, you might Google the confirmation address to verify its existence.

Agree the confirmed bank balance to the period-end bank reconciliation (e.g., December 31, 20X7). Then, agree the reconciling items on the bank reconciliation to the subsequent period bank statement. For example, examine the January 20X8 bank statement activity when clearing the December 20X7 reconciling items. Finally, agree the reconciled balance to the general ledger.

The auditor might examine the reconciling items by viewing online bank statements. (Read-only rights can be given to the auditor.)

I don't normally test cash controls (e.g., test of bank reconciliation controls) for effectiveness, but you do have that option. If such controls are tested and you determine they are effective, then some of the substantive tests listed above may not be necessary.

Common Cash Work Papers

My cash work papers normally include the following:

- An understanding of cash-related internal controls
- Risk assessment of cash at the assertion level
- Documentation of any control deficiencies
- Cash audit program
- Bank reconciliations for each significant account
- Bank confirmations
- Disclosure checklist

Auditing Cash - A Simple Summary

- The primary relevant cash assertions include existence, completeness, rights, accuracy, and cutoff
- Perform a walkthrough of cash by making inquiries, inspecting documents, and making observations
- The directional risk for cash is that it is overstated
- Primary risks for cash include:
  - Cash is stolen
  - Cash is intentionally overstated to cover up theft
  - Cash accounts are intentionally omitted from the general ledger
  - Cash is misstated due to errors in the bank reconciliation
  - Cash is misstated due to improper cutoff
- The substantive procedures for cash should be responsive to the identified risks. Common procedures include:
  - Confirmation of cash
  - Vouching reconciling items to the subsequent month's bank statement

- Asking if all bank accounts are included in the general ledger
- Inspecting period-end deposits and disbursements for proper cutoff

Now you know how to audit cash. Next we'll see how to audit receivables and revenues.

CHAPTER 6
The Why and How of
Auditing Receivables/Revenue

———

Revenues are the lifeblood of any organization. Without cash inflows, the entity may cease to exist. So, it's important that businesses generate sales or some type of revenue.

For you, the auditor, it's important to verify revenue and related receivables. Why? Because some companies manipulate their earnings by inflating their receivables. When trade receivables increase, revenues increase. A company can fraudulently increase its net income by recording nonexistent or inflated receivables.

In this chapter, we'll answer questions such as, "Should I confirm receivables or examine subsequent receipts?" and "Why should I assume that revenues are overstated?"

Auditing Receivable and Revenues — An Overview

In this chapter, we will cover the following:

- Primary accounts receivable and revenue assertions
- Accounts receivable and revenue walkthrough
- Directional risk for accounts receivable and revenues
- Primary risks for accounts receivable and revenues
- Common accounts receivable and revenue control deficiencies
- Risk of material misstatement for accounts receivable and revenues
- Substantive procedures for accounts receivable and revenues
- Common accounts receivable and revenue work papers

Primary Accounts Receivable and Revenue Assertions

First, let's look at assertions. The primary relevant accounts receivable and revenue assertions include:

- Existence and occurrence
- Completeness
- Accuracy
- Valuation
- Cutoff

Of these assertions, I believe—in general—existence of receivables, occurrence of revenues, cutoff of receivables and revenues, and valuation of receivables are most important. Clients assert that receivables exist, that receivables and revenues are recorded in the right period, that revenues occurred, and that receivables are properly valued. Additionally, accuracy comes into play if the customer has complex receivable transactions. Though usually less of a risk, the completeness assertion can be relevant when a company fails to properly record its receivables.

Accounts Receivable and Revenue Walkthrough

Second, perform your risk assessment work in light of the potential relevant assertions. In performing accounts receivable and revenue walkthroughs, ask questions such as:

- Are receivable subsidiary ledgers reconciled to the general ledger?
- Is a consistent allowance methodology used?
- What method is used to compute the allowance and is it reasonable?
- Who records and approves the allowance?
- Who reviews aged receivables?
- What controls ensure that revenues are recorded in the right period?
- Is there proper segregation of duties between persons

recording, billing, and collecting payments? Who reconciles the related records?

- What software is used to track billings and collections?
- Are there any decentralized collection locations?
- When are revenues recognized and is the recognition in accordance with the reporting framework?
- What receivables and revenue reports are provided to the owners or the governing body?

As we ask questions, we also inspect documents (e.g., aged receivable reports) and make observations (e.g., who collects the payments).

If control weaknesses exist, we create audit procedures to respond to them. For example, if—during the walkthrough—we see inconsistent allowance methods, we will perform more substantive work in relation to the allowance account.

Directional Risk for Accounts Receivable and Revenues

Third, consider the directional risk of accounts receivable and revenues. The directional risk for accounts receivable and revenue is that they are overstated. In performing your audit procedures, ensure that accounts receivables and revenues are not overstated. For example, review the cutoff procedures. Be sure that no subsequent period revenues are recorded in the current fiscal year.

Audit standards require that auditors review estimates for management bias. So, consider the current year allowance and bad debt write-offs in light of the prior year allowance. This retrospective review allows the auditor to see if the estimate is biased. There is a threat that management might reduce allowances to inflate earnings.

Moreover, the audit standards state there is a presumption (unless rebutted) that revenues are overstated. Therefore, we are to assume revenues are overstated, unless we can explain why they are not.

Primary Risks for Accounts Receivable and Revenues

Fourth, think about the risks related to receivables and revenues. The main risks include:

- An intentional overstatement of accounts receivable and revenue
- Theft of collections
- Overstated accounts receivable and revenue due to improper cutoff
- Understated allowances
- Inconsistent or improper revenue recognition

Risks related to revenue vary from company to company. For example, one telecommunications company might sell bundled services while another may not. Revenue recognition is more complex (risky) for the company selling bundled services.

Also, risk related to revenue varies from industry to industry. For example, the allowance for uncollectible is a high risk area for healthcare entities, but may not be in other industries.

Common Accounts Receivable and Revenue Control Deficiencies

Fifth, think about the control deficiencies noted during your walkthroughs and other risk assessment work.

In smaller entities, the following control deficiencies are common:

- One person performs two or more of the following:
  - Bills customers
  - Receipts monies
  - Makes deposits
  - Records those payments, and
  - Reconciles the related bank account

- The person computing allowances doesn't possess sufficient knowledge to do so
- No surprise audits of receivables and revenues
- Multiple people work from one cash drawer
- Receipts are not appropriately issued
- Receipts are not reconciled to daily collections
- Daily receipts are not reviewed by a second person
- No one reconciles subsidiary receivable ledgers to the general ledger
- Individuals with the ability to adjust customer receivable accounts also collect cash (and a second person is not monitoring adjustments)
- Inconsistent bad debt recognition with no second-person review
- The revenue recognition policy may not be clear and may not be in accordance with the reporting framework

Risk of Material Misstatement for Accounts Receivable and Revenues

Sixth, assess your risks of material misstatement in light of the information you've gathered.

The assertions that concern me the most are existence, cutoff, occurrence, and valuation. So my RMM for these assertions is usually moderate to high.

My response to higher risk assessments is to perform certain substantive procedures: namely, receivable confirmations and tests of subsequent collections. As RMM increases, I send more confirmations and examine more subsequent collections.

Additionally, I thoroughly test management's allowance computation. I pay particular attention to uncollected amounts beyond 90 days. Uncollected amounts beyond 90 days should usually be heavily reserved. And amounts beyond 120 days should—in most cases—be fully reserved.

Substantive Procedures for Accounts Receivable and Revenues

And finally, it's time to determine your substantive procedures in light of your identified risks.

My customary audit procedures are as follows:

- Confirm accounts receivable balances (especially larger amounts)
- Vouch subsequent period collections, making sure the subsequent collections relate to the period-end balances (sampling can be used)
- Review allowance computations to see if they are consistent with prior years, compare allowance percentages to industry averages, agree the allowance to supporting documentation (e.g., histories of uncollectible amounts), and recompute the related numbers
- Compare all significant revenue accounts with historical data (three or more years if possible)
- Create summaries of average customer income (e.g., total revenue by category divided by the number of customers) and compare with prior periods
- Compute average profit margins by sales categories and compare with previous years

If you identify a risk of theft, perform related substantive procedures. For example, you might examine write-offs of receivables for employees that handle cash.

Controls can be tested for billing, collection, and posting. If controls are effective, then some substantive procedures may not be necessary.

Common Accounts Receivable and Revenue Work Papers

My accounts receivable and revenue work papers usually include the following:

- An understanding of accounts receivable and revenue-related internal controls
- Risk assessment of accounts receivable and revenue at the assertion level
- Documentation of any control deficiencies
- Accounts receivable and revenue audit program
- An aged receivables detail at period-end
- Copies of receivable confirmations
- A summary of confirmations received
- Subsequent collection work papers
- Allowance work paper
- Revenue comparison work papers
- Disclosure checklist

Auditing Receivables/Revenue - A Simple Summary

- Primary relevant receivable/revenue assertions include existence of receivables, cutoff of receivables and revenues, occurrence of revenues, and valuation of receivables
- Perform a walkthrough of the receivables/revenue cycle by making inquiries, inspecting documents, and making observations
- The directional risk for receivables and revenue is that they are overstated
- Primary risks for receivables and revenues include:
  - An intentional overstatement of accounts receivable and revenue
  - Theft of collections
  - Overstated accounts receivable and revenue due to improper cutoff
  - Understated allowances

    – Inconsistent or improper revenue recognition
- The substantive procedures for receivables and revenue should be responsive to the identified risks. Common procedures include:
  - Confirmation of accounts receivable balances
  - Vouching subsequent period collections
  - Reviewing allowance computations to see if they are consistent with prior years and appropriate for the current year
  - Comparing all significant revenue accounts with historical data
  - Creating summaries of average customer income (e.g., total revenue by category divided by the number of customers) and comparing with prior years
  - Computing average profit margins by sales categories and comparing with previous years
  - Fraud-related procedures such as examining write-offs of receivables for employees handling cash

Now you know how to audit receivables and revenues.

Next, we'll see how to audit investments.

CHAPTER 7
The Why and How of Auditing Investments

—————

The complexity of auditing investments varies. For entities with simple investment instruments, auditing is easy. Your main audit procedure might be to confirm balances. Complex investments, however, require additional work such as auditing values. As investment complexity increases, so will your need for stronger audit team members. Regardless, you need an audit methodology.

How to Audit Investments

In this chapter, we will take a look at:

- Primary investment assertions
- Investment walkthroughs
- Directional risk for investments
- Primary risks for investments
- Common investment control deficiencies
- Risk of material misstatement for investments
- Substantive procedures for investments
- Common investment work papers

Primary Investments Assertions

First, let's look at assertions.

Primary relevant investment assertions include:

- Existence
- Accuracy

- Valuation
- Cutoff
- Completeness

The audit client asserts that the investment balances exist, that they are accurate and properly valued, and that only investment activity within the period is recorded.

While investment balances in the financial statements are important, disclosures are also vital, especially when the entity owns complex instruments. Thus, the completeness and accuracy assertions are relevant.

Investment Walkthroughs

Second, perform your risk assessment work in light of the potential relevant assertions. In performing investment walkthroughs, ask questions such as:

- What types of investments are owned?
- Are there any unusual investments? If yes, how are they valued?
- Is a specialist used to determine investment values?
- Who determines the classification of investments (i.e., trading, available for sale, held to maturity) and how?
- Do the persons accounting for investment activity have sufficient knowledge to do so?
- Are timely investment reconciliations performed by competent personnel?
- Are *all* investment accounts reconciled from the investment statements to the general ledger?
- Who reconciles the investment accounts and when?
- Are the reconciliations reviewed by a second person?
- Are all investment accounts on the general ledger?
- How does the entity ensure that all investment activity is included in the general ledger (appropriate cutoff)?

- Who has the ability to transfer investment funds and what are the related controls?
- Is there appropriate segregation of duties for:
  - Persons that record investments,
  - Persons that buy and sell investments, and
  - Persons that reconcile the investment statements?
- What investment accounts were opened in the period?
- What investment accounts were closed in the period?
- Who has the authority to open or close investment accounts?
- Are there any investment restrictions (externally or internally)?
- What persons are authorized to buy and sell investments?
- Does the entity have a written investment policy?
- Does the company use an investment advisor? If yes, how often does management interact with the advisor? How are investment fees determined?
- Are there any investment impairments?
- Who is responsible for investment disclosures and do they have sufficient knowledge to carry out this duty?
- Are there any cost or equity-method investments?

As we ask questions, we also inspect documents such as investment statements and make observations such as who reconciles the investment statements to the general ledger.

If control weaknesses exist, we create audit procedures to address them. For example, if during the walkthrough we note that there are improperly classified investments, then we will create audit procedures to address that risk.

Directional Risk for Investments

Third, consider the directional risk of investments. The directional risk for investments is that they are overstated. So, in performing your audit procedures, perform procedures to ensure that balances are properly stated.

Primary Risks for Investments

Fourth, think about the risks related to investments. Primary risks include:

- Investments are stolen
- Investments are intentionally overstated to cover up theft
- Investment accounts are intentionally omitted from the general ledger
- Investments are misstated due to errors in the investment reconciliations
- Investments are improperly valued due to management's lack of knowledge regarding accounting standards and the investments themselves
- Investments are misstated due to improper cutoff
- Investment disclosures are not accurate or complete

Common Investment Control Deficiencies

Fifth, think about control deficiencies noted during your walkthroughs and other risk assessment work. It is common to have the following investment control deficiencies:

- One person buys and sells investments, records those transactions, and reconciles the investment activity
- The person overseeing investment accounting does not possess sufficient knowledge or skill to properly perform the duty
- Investment reconciliations are not performed timely or improperly
- The company does not employ sufficient assistance in valuing complex assets such as hedges or alternative investments

Risk of Material Misstatement for Investments

Sixth, assess your risks of material misstatement with the information you've gathered.

The assertions that concern me the most are existence, accuracy, valuation, cutoff, and completeness. So my RMM for these assertions is usually moderate to high.

Substantive Procedures for Investments

And finally, it's time to determine your substantive procedures in light of your identified risks.

My customary audit tests include:

- Confirming investment balances and agreeing them to the general ledger
- Inspecting period-end activity for proper cutoff
- Using an investment specialist to value complex instruments (if any)
- Vetting investment disclosures with a current disclosure checklist

I don't normally test controls related to investments. If controls are tested and you determine they are effective, then some of the substantive procedures may not be necessary.

Common Investment Work Papers

My investment work papers normally include the following:

- An understanding of investment-related internal controls
- Risk assessment of investments at the assertion level
- Documentation of any control deficiencies
- Investment audit program
- Investment reconciliations
- Investment confirmations
- Valuations performed by specialists
- Documentation of the specialist's experience, competence, and objectivity
- Disclosure checklist

Auditing Investments - A Simple Summary

- The primary relevant investment assertions include existence, accuracy, valuation, cutoff, and completeness
- Perform a walkthrough of investments by making inquiries, inspecting documents, and making observations
- The directional risk for investments is an overstatement
- Primary risks for investments include:
  - Investments are stolen
  - Investments are intentionally overstated to cover up theft
  - Investment accounts are intentionally omitted from the general ledger
  - Investments are misstated due to errors in the investment reconciliations
  - Investments are improperly valued due to management's lack of knowledge regarding accounting standards and the investments themselves
  - Investments are misstated due to improper cutoff
  - Investments disclosures are not accurate or complete
- The substantive procedures for investments should be responsive to the identified risks. Common procedures include:
  - Confirming investments
  - Inspecting period-end activity for proper cutoff
  - Using an investment specialist to value complex instruments
  - Vetting investment disclosures with a current disclosure checklist

Now you know how to audit investments.

Next, we'll see how to audit property

CHAPTER 8

The Why and How of Auditing Property

———

Plant, property, and equipment is often the largest item on a balance sheet. But the risk is usually low to moderate. After all, it's difficult to steal land or a building. And the accounting is usually not difficult. So the dollar amount can be high but the risk low.

In this chapter, we'll answer questions such as, "How should we test additions of property?" and "What should we do in regard to fair value impairments?"

Auditing Property — An Overview

I will refer to plant, property, and equipment as *property*.

Property is purchased for use in a business. For example, a corporate office might be bought or constructed. The building is an asset that is depreciated over its economic life. As depreciation is recorded, the book value (cost less accumulated depreciation) decreases. In other words, you expense the building as it is used.

In most reporting frameworks, assets are recorded at cost. Appreciation in the value of property is not recorded, but a significant decrease, known as an impairment, is recognized. Property improvements (e.g., adding a new room to an existing building) are capitalized and depreciated. Repairs like painting a room are not. They are expensed as incurred.

Also, most businesses elect to use a capitalization threshold such as $5,000. For these entities, amounts paid below the threshold are not capitalized, even if they extend the life of the asset. Such amounts are expensed as incurred.

How do most entities track property purchases and compute the related depreciation? They use depreciation software. When property is purchased, it is added to the depreciation software and an economic life (e.g., ten years) is assigned. Thereafter, the cost and depreciation are maintained in the software. Journal entries are made in the general ledger to record the depreciation for each period.

Below we will cover the following:

- Primary property assertions
- Property walkthroughs
- Directional risk for property
- Primary risks for property
- Common property control deficiencies
- Risk of material misstatement for property
- Substantive procedures for property
- Common property work papers

Primary Property Assertions

First, let's look at assertions.

The primary relevant property assertions include:

- Existence and occurrence
- Completeness
- Valuation
- Classification

Of these assertions, I believe existence, occurrence, and classification are generally most important. The client is asserting that property exists, that depreciation expense is appropriate, and that amounts paid for property are capitalized (and not expensed). If the value of a property is significantly impaired, then the valuation assertion is relevant.

Property Walkthroughs

Second, perform your risk assessment work in light of the potential relevant assertions.

In performing the walkthrough, ask questions such as:

- Are property ledgers reconciled to the general ledger?
- Does the entity use reasonable and consistent depreciation methods?
- Are the depreciation methods in accordance with the reporting framework?
- Who records depreciation?
- Are the economic lives assigned to property appropriate?
- What controls ensure that property is recorded in the right period?
- Is there appropriate segregation of duties between persons who purchase, record, reconcile, and physically possess property?
- What software is used to compute depreciation?
- Does the company perform periodic physical inventories of property?
- Are assets removed from the depreciation schedule and the general ledger upon sale?
- What controls ensure that property purchases are added to the depreciation schedule (and not expensed as repairs and maintenance)?
- What controls ensure that repair expenses are not capitalized as property?
- What is the capitalization threshold (e.g., $5,000)?
- Is there a written policy for bidding purchases?
- How are bids reviewed and documented?
- Is there a written policy for disposal of assets?

As we ask questions, we also inspect documents (e.g., depreciation reports) and make observations (e.g., who has access to moveable property?).

If control weaknesses exist, we create audit procedures to respond to them. For example, if—during the walkthrough—we see that one person purchases property, has physical access to equipment, and performs the related accounting, then we will perform theft-related substantive procedures.

Directional Risk for Property

Third, consider the directional risk of property. The directional risk for property is that is is overstated. So, in performing your audit procedures, perform procedures to ensure that property is not overstated. For example, vouch all significant property additions to invoices. See if the amounts added to property are equal to or greater than the capitalization threshold (e.g., $5,000).

Primary Risks for Property

Fourth, think about the risks related to property. The primary risks for property include:

- Property is intentionally overstated
- Repair expenses (or any other expenses) are improperly capitalized
- Purchases that should be recorded as property are expensed
- Depreciation is improperly computed and recorded (e.g., accelerated depreciation is used when straight-line is more appropriate)
- Moveable property like equipment is stolen
- Those with purchasing power receive kickbacks from outside parties (e.g., vendors)

Common Property Control Deficiencies

Fifth, think about control deficiencies noted during your walkthroughs and other risk assessment work.

In smaller entities, it is common to have the following control deficiencies:

- One person performs more than one of the following:
  - Authorizes the purchase of property
  - Records the property in the general ledger and depreciation schedule
  - Has physical custody of the property
  - Has responsibility for reconciling the depreciation schedule to the general ledger
- The person maintaining depreciation records lacks the knowledge to do so
- A second person does not review the depreciation methods for appropriateness and economic lives assigned to each property
- No one performs surprise audits of property
- No one performs physical inventories of property
- There are no controls over the disposal of property
- Appropriate bidding procedures are not used
- No one reconciles the depreciation schedule to the general ledger
- Property is not reviewed for potential impairments of value

Risk of Material Misstatement for Property

Sixth, assess your risks of material misstatement with the information you've gathered.

The assertions that concern me the most are existence for additions to property, occurrence for depreciation, and classification of property. With regard to classification, the business determines whether the amount should be capitalized or expensed. My RMM for these assertions is usually moderate to high.

My response to higher risk assessments is to perform certain substantive procedures: namely, vouching additions to property. (Vouching means to compare property additions to invoices paid.) As RMM increases, I use a lower dollar threshold for vouching.

If controls related to bids are weak, your RMM for existence can be high. Bid rigging or kickbacks (fraudulent vendor actions) can result in overstatements of property.

Substantive Procedures for Property

Finally, it's time to determine your substantive procedures in light of your identified risks.

My customary audit tests are as follows:

- Vouch property additions to related invoices
- Agree opening property balances in the depreciation schedule to the prior year ending balances
- Review economic lives assigned to new property for appropriateness
- Review the selected depreciation method in light of the property's economic life—does the property lose value quickly or evenly over time?
- Compute a ratio of depreciation to property and compare the result with prior periods
- Inquire about potential decreases in the value of property and request valuations if necessary
- Review significant bid documentation

I don't normally test controls related to property. If controls are tested and you determine they are effective, then some of the substantive procedures may not be necessary.

Common Property Work Papers

My property work papers normally include the following:

- An understanding of property-related internal controls
- Risk assessment of property at the assertion level
- Documentation of control deficiencies related to property
- Property audit program

- A copy of the depreciation schedule that agrees to the general ledger
- A summary of additions and retirements of property in the current audit period
- Bid documents for significant construction projects or other property purchases
- A valuation of a significant asset by a valuation specialist, if needed
- Disclosure checklist

Auditing Property - A Simple Summary

- Primary relevant property assertions include existence for property, occurrence for depreciation, and classification with regard to whether the amount should be capitalized or expensed.
- Perform a walkthrough of the property cycle by making inquiries, inspecting documents, and making observations
- The directional risk for property is that it is overstated
- Primary risks for property include:
  - Property is intentionally overstated
  - Repair expenses are improperly capitalized
  - Purchases that should be recorded as property are expensed
  - Depreciation is improperly computed and recorded
  - Moveable property is stolen
  - Those with purchasing power receive kickbacks from outside parties (e.g., vendors)
- The substantive procedures for property should be responsive to the identified risks. Common procedures include:
  - Vouching property additions to related invoices
  - Agreeing opening property balances in the depreciation schedule to the prior year ending balances
  - Reviewing economic lives assigned to new property for appropriateness

- Reviewing the selected depreciation method in light of the property's economic life
- Computing a ratio of depreciation to property and comparing the result with prior periods
- Inquiring about potential decreases in the value of property and requesting valuations if necessary
- Review significant bid documentation

Now you know how to audit property.

Next we'll turn our attention to the audit of accounts payable and expenses.

CHAPTER 9

The Why and How of
Auditing Payables/Expenses

Accounts payable is usually one of the more important audit areas. Why? Risk. First, it's easy to increase net income by not recording period-end payables. Second, many forms of theft occur in this area.

In this chapter, we'll answer questions such as, "How should we test accounts payable?" And "Should we perform fraud-related expense procedures?" We'll also take a look at common accounts payable risks and how to respond to them.

Auditing Accounts Payable and Expenses — An Overview

What is a payable? It's the amount that a company owes for services or goods received. Suppose a company receives $2,000 in legal services in the last week of December 20X3, but the law firm sends the related invoice in January 20X4. The company owes $2,000 as of December 31, 20X3. The services were provided, but the payment was not made until after the year-end. Consequently, the company should accrue the $2,000 as payable at year-end.

In determining whether payables exist, I like to ask, "If the company closed down at midnight on the last day of the year, would it have a legal obligation to pay for a service or good?" If the answer is yes, then record the payable even if the invoice is received after the year-end.

In this chapter, we will cover the following:

- Primary accounts payable and expense assertions
- Accounts payable and expense walkthroughs
- Directional risk for accounts payable and expenses
- Primary risks for accounts payable and expenses
- Common accounts payable and expense control deficiencies
- Risks of material misstatement for accounts payable and expenses
- Substantive procedures for accounts payable and expenses
- Common accounts payable and expense work papers

Primary Accounts Payable and Expense Assertions

First, let's look at assertions. The primary relevant accounts payable and expense assertions include:

- Existence
- Completeness
- Cutoff
- Occurrence

Of these assertions, I believe completeness for payables and expenses, cutoff for payables and expenses, and occurrence for expenses are usually most important. When a company records its payables and expenses by period-end, it is asserting that they are complete and that they are accounted for in the right period. Additionally, the company is implying that recorded expenses are legitimate, i.e., that they occurred.

Accounts Payable and Expense Walkthroughs

Second, perform your risk assessment work in light of the potential relevant assertions. In performing accounts payable and expense walkthroughs, ask questions such as:

- Who reconciles the accounts payable summary to the general ledger?
- Does the company use an annual expense budget?
- Are budget/expense reports provided to management or others? Who receives those reports?
- What controls ensure the recording of payables in the appropriate period?
- Who authorizes purchase orders? Are any purchases authorized by means other than a purchase order? If yes, how?
- Are purchase orders electronic or physical?
- Are purchase orders numbered?
- How does the company vet new vendors?
- Who codes invoices (specifies the expense account) and how?
- Is a three-way match performed that is a comparison of the purchase order with the receiving document and the invoice?
- Are paid invoices marked "paid"?
- Does the company have a purchasing policy?
- Can credit cards be used to bypass standard purchasing procedures? Who has credit cards and what are the limits? Who reviews credit card activity?
- Are bids required for certain types of purchases or dollar amounts? Who administers the bidding process and how?
- Do larger payments require multiple approvals?
- Which employees key invoices into the accounts payable software?
- Who signs checks or makes electronic payments?
- Who is on the bank signature card?
- Are signature stamps used? If yes, who has control of the signature stamps and whose signature is affixed?

- How are electronic payments made (e.g., ACH)?
- Is there adequate segregation of duties for persons approving purchases, making payments, recording payables, and reconciling the related bank statements
- Which persons have access to check stock and where is the check stock stored?
- Who can add vendors to the payables system?
- What are the entity's procedures for payments of travel and entertainment expenses?
- Who reconciles the bank statements and how often?
- Are payees on cleared checks compared to the general ledger postings?

As we ask these questions, we inspect documents (e.g., payables ledger) and make observations (e.g., who signs checks or makes electronic payments?).

If control weaknesses exist, we create audit procedures to respond to them. For example, if—during the walkthrough— we see that one person prints and signs checks, records payments, and reconciles the bank statement, then we will perform fraud-related substantive procedures.

Directional Risk for Accounts Payable and Expenses

Third, consider the directional risk of accounts payable and expenses.

The directional risk for accounts payable and expenses is that they are understated. Perform procedures to ensure that invoices are properly included. For example, perform a search for unrecorded liabilities, as detailed below.

Primary Risks for Accounts Payable and Expenses

Fourth, think about the risks related to accounts payable and expenses. The primary risks for accounts payable and expenses include:

- Accounts payable and expenses are intentionally understated
- Payments are made to inappropriate parties
- Duplicate payments are made to vendors
- Inflated amounts are paid to vendors (after company employees receive kickbacks)
- Management does not follow bid policy requirements

Common Accounts Payable and Expense Control Deficiencies

Fifth, think about control deficiencies noted during your walkthroughs and other risk assessment work. In smaller entities, it is common to have the following control deficiencies:

- One person performs two or more of the following:
    - Approves purchases
    - Enters invoices in the accounts payable system
    - Issues checks or makes electronic payments
    - Reconciles the accounts payable bank account
    - Adds new vendors to the accounts payable system
- A second person does not review payments before issuance
- No one performs surprise audits of accounts payable and expenses
- Bidding procedures are weak or absent
- No one reconciles the accounts payable detail to the general ledger
- New vendors are not vetted for appropriateness
- The company does not create a budget
- No one compares expenses to the budget

- Bank accounts are not reconciled on a timely basis
- When bank accounts are reconciled, no one examines the canceled checks for appropriate payees (no one compares the payee name on the cleared check to the vendor name in the general ledger)

When segregation of duties is lacking, consider whether someone can use the expense cycle to steal funds. How? Examples include making payments to fictitious vendors or intentionally paying a vendor twice—and then stealing the second check.

Risks of Material Misstatement for Accounts Payable and Expenses

Sixth, assess the risks of material misstatement in light of the information you've gathered.

The assertions that concern me the most are completeness, occurrence, and cutoff. So my RMM for these assertions is usually moderate to high.

My response to higher risk assessments is to perform certain substantive procedures: namely, a search for unrecorded liabilities and detailed expense analyses. The particular expense accounts that I examine are often the result of my preliminary planning analytics. (See Appendix A for a detailed look at preliminary analytics.)

Substantive Procedures for Accounts Payable and Expenses

And finally, it's time to determine your substantive procedures in light of your identified risks.

My customary audit tests are as follows:

- Perform a search for unrecorded liabilities
- Compare expenses to budget or prior year balances and

examine any unexplained variances
- When control weaknesses are present, consider designing and performing fraud detection procedures

Controls can be tested for accounts payable processing. If controls are effective, then some substantive procedures may not be necessary.

How does one perform a search for unrecorded liabilities? Perform the following steps:

1. Obtain a complete check register for the period subsequent to your audit period
2. Pick a dollar threshold in light of materiality (e.g., $5,000)
3. Examine the subsequent payments (above the threshold) and related invoices to determine if the payables are suitably included in or excluded from the period-end accounts payable detail
4. Inquire about any unrecorded invoices

As the RMM for completeness increases, vouch payments at a lower dollar threshold.

How should you perform a detailed analysis of expense accounts? First, compare the expenses to budget—if the entity has one—or to prior year balances. If you note any significant variances that can't be explained, then obtain a detail of those particular expense accounts and investigate the cause.

Theft can occur in numerous ways such as fictitious vendors or duplicate payments. If control weaknesses are present, consider performing fraud-related procedures. When fraud-related control weaknesses exist, assess the RMM for the occurrence assertion at high. Why? There is a risk that the expense (the occurrence) is fraudulent.

An example of a fraud-related test is one for duplicate payments. How?

- Obtain a check register in Excel
- Sort by the vendor
- Scan the check register for payments made to the same vendor for the same amount
- Inquire about payments made to the same vendor for the same amount

In a duplicate payment fraud, the thief intentionally pays an invoice twice. He steals the second check and converts it to cash. This is just one example of expense fraud. There are dozens of such schemes.

If there are going concern issues, you may need to examine the aged payables listing. Why? Management can fraudulently shorten invoice due dates. Doing so makes the company appear more current. For example, suppose the business has three unpaid invoices totaling $1.3 million that are more than ninety days past due. The company changes the due dates in the accounts payable system, causing the invoices to appear as though they are just thirty days past due. Now the aged payables listing looks better than it should.

Common Accounts Payable and Expense Work Papers

My accounts payable and expense work papers usually include the following:

- An understanding of internal controls as they relate to accounts payable and expenses
- Risk assessment of accounts payable and expenses at the assertion level
- Documentation of any accounts payable and expense control deficiencies

- Accounts payable and expense audit program
- An aged accounts payable detail at period-end
- A search for unrecorded liabilities work paper
- Budget to actual (or prior year to current year) expense reports and, if unexpected variances are noted, a detailed analysis of those accounts
- Fraud-related expense work papers (if significant control weaknesses are present)
- Disclosure checklist

Auditing Payables/Expenses - A Simple Summary

- Primary relevant assertions include completeness and cutoff for payables and expenses and occurrence for expenses
- Perform a walkthrough of the payables/expenses cycle by making inquiries, inspecting documents, and making observations
- The directional risk for payables and expenses is that they are understated
- Primary risks for payables/expenses include:
  - Accounts payable and expenses are intentionally understated
  - Payments are made to inappropriate parties
  - Duplicate payments are made to vendors
  - Inflated amounts are paid to vendors
  - Management does not follow bid policy requirements
- The substantive procedures for payables and expenses should be responsive to the identified risks. Common procedures include:
  - Performing a search for unrecorded liabilities
  - Comparing expenses to budget (or prior year balances) and examining any unexplained variances
  - When control weaknesses are present, designing and performing fraud detection procedures

Now you know how to audit accounts payable and expenses. Next we'll turn our attention to the audit of payroll.

CHAPTER 10
The Why and How of Auditing Payroll

While payroll is often seen as a low-risk area, considerable losses can occur here. Knowing how to audit payroll is important. In this chapter, I'll answer questions such as, "How should I test payroll?", and, "When should I perform fraud-related payroll procedures?"

Auditing Payroll - An Overview

Payroll exceeds fifty percent of total expenses in many governments, nonprofits, and small businesses. Therefore, it is often a significant transaction area.

To assist you in understanding how to audit payroll, let me provide you with an overview of a typical payroll process.

First, understand that entities have payroll cycles (e.g., two weeks starting on Monday). Then, payments are made after the period-end (e.g., the Tuesday after the two-week period). Also, understand that most organizations have salaried and hourly employees. Salaried personnel are paid a standard amount each payroll, and hourly employees earn their wages based on time.

Second, an authorized person (e.g., department head) hires a new employee at a specified rate (e.g., $80,000 per year).

Third, human resources assists the new-hire with the completion of payroll forms, including tax and benefit documents.

Fourth, a payroll department employee enters the approved wage in the accounting system. Also, the employee's bank account number is entered into the system (if direct deposit is used).

Fifth, employees clock in and out so that time can be recorded.

Sixth, once the payroll period is complete, a departmental supervisor reviews and approves the recorded time.

Seventh, a payroll supervisor approves the overall payroll.

Eighth, the payroll department processes payments. Direct deposit payments are made (and everyone is happy).

In this chapter, we will cover the following:

- Primary payroll assertions
- Payroll walkthroughs
- Directional risk for payroll
- Primary risks for payroll
- Common payroll control deficiencies
- Risk of material misstatement for payroll
- Substantive procedures for payroll
- Common payroll work papers

Primary Payroll Assertions

First, let's look at assertions. The primary relevant payroll assertions include:

- Completeness
- Cutoff
- Occurrence
- Classification
- Accuracy

I believe—in general—completeness and cutoff for accrued payroll liabilities and occurrence for payroll expenses are the most important payroll assertions. When a company accrues payroll liabilities at period-end, it is asserting that they are complete and that they are recorded in the right period. Additionally, the company is saying that recorded payroll expenses are legitimate.

When a company offers defined benefit pension plans or other postretirement benefits, the classification assertion is usually relevant. The accuracy and completeness assertions are relevant with regard to amounts reflected in the financial statements and the related disclosures.

Payroll Walkthroughs

Second, perform your risk assessment work in light of the potential relevant assertions. Walk transactions from the beginning (the hiring of an employee) to the end (a payroll payment and posting). And ask questions such as the following:

- Does the company have a separate payroll bank account?
- How often is payroll processed? What time period does the payroll cover? On what day is payroll paid?
- Who has the authority to hire and fire employees?
- What paperwork is required for a new employee? For a terminated employee?
- Is payroll budgeted?
- Who monitors the budget to actual reports? How often?
- Who controls payroll check stock? Where is it stored? Is it secure?
- If the company uses direct deposit, who keys the bank account numbers into the payroll system? Who can change those numbers?
- Do larger salary payments require multiple approvals?
- Who approves overtime payments?
- Who monitors compliance with payroll laws and regulations?
- Who processes payroll and how?
- Who signs checks or makes electronic payments? If physical

checks are used, are they signed electronically (as checks are printed) or physically?

- How are payroll tax payments made? How often? Who makes them?
- Who creates the year-end payroll tax documents (e.g., W-2s) and how? Who creates quarterly tax returns and how?
- What controls ensure the recording of payroll in the appropriate period?
- Are the following duties assigned to different persons:
  - Approval of payroll
  - Processing and recording payroll
  - Signing payroll checks
  - The reconciliation of related bank statements
  - Possession of processed payroll checks
  - Ability to enter or change employee bank account numbers
  - Ability to add employees to the payroll system or to remove them
- Who can add or remove employees from the payroll system? What is the process for adding and removing employees from the payroll system?
- Who can change the master pay rate file? Does the computer system provide an audit trail of those changes, including who made them?
- Who approves salary rates and how?
- Who reconciles the payroll bank statements and how often?
- Who approves bonuses?
- What benefits does the company offer? Who pays for the benefits and how? Is there a plan document? Do the accounting personnel understand the related accounting standards and requirements? What controls are used to ensure proper benefit plan accounting?
- Who reconciles the payroll withholding accounts and how often?

- Are any salaries capitalized rather than expensed? If yes, how and why?
- Are surprise payroll audits performed? If yes, by whom?
- Does the company outsource its payroll to a service organization? If yes, does the payroll company provide a service organization control (SOC) report? What are the service organization controls? What are the complementary controls, i.e., those performed by the employing company?

Moreover, as we ask these questions, we need to inspect documents like the payroll ledger and make observations, like who signs checks or makes electronic payments.

If control weaknesses exist, we create audit procedures to respond to them. For example, during the walkthrough, if we see that one person prints and signs checks, records payments, and reconciles the bank statement, then we will plan fraud-related substantive procedures.

As we perform payroll walkthroughs, we are asking, "What can go wrong—whether intentionally or by mistake?"

When payroll fraud occurs, understatements or overstatements of payroll expense may exist. If a company desires to inflate its profit, it can—using bookkeeping tricks—understate its expenses. As reported costs go down, profits go up. On the other hand, overstatements of payroll can occur when theft is present. For example, if a payroll accountant pays himself twice, payroll expenses are higher than they should be.

Mistakes also lead to payroll misstatements. Payroll errors can occur when payroll personnel lack sufficient knowledge to carry out their duties. Additionally, misstatements occur when employees fail to perform internal control procedures such as reconciling bank statements.

Directional Risk for Payroll

Third, consider the directional risk of payroll. The directional risk for payroll is an understatement. Make sure you audit for completeness (determining that all payroll and benefits are recorded). Nevertheless, when payroll theft occurs, such as duplicate payments, overstatements can occur.

Primary Risks for Payroll

Fourth, think about the risks related to payroll.

The primary payroll risks include:

- Payroll is intentionally understated to inflate profits
- Inappropriate parties receive payments
- Employees receive duplicate payments
- Employees receive inflated payments
- Pensions and other postretirement benefits are improperly recorded or disclosed

Common Payroll Control Deficiencies

Fifth, think about control deficiencies noted during your walkthroughs and other risk assessment work.

In smaller entities, it is common to have the following control deficiencies:

- One person performs two or more of the following:
  - Approves payroll payments to employees
  - Enters time or salary rates in the payroll system
  - Signs payroll checks or makes direct deposit payments
  - Adds or removes employees from the payroll system
  - Reconciles the payroll bank account
- No one reviews and approves recorded time
- No one reviews and approves payroll before processing
- No one performs surprise audits of payroll

- Appropriate procedures for adding and removing employees are not present
- No one reviews the removal of terminated employees from payroll
- No one compares payroll expenses to budget
- Accounting personnel lack sufficient knowledge with regard to pensions and other postretirement benefits
- Pension and other postretirement benefit accounting controls are lacking

Risk of Material Misstatement for Payroll

Sixth, assess your risk of material misstatement with the information you've gathered.

In auditing payroll, the assertions that concern me the most are completeness, cutoff, and occurrence. So my risk of material misstatement for these assertions is usually moderate to high.

My response to higher risk assessments is to perform certain substantive procedures: namely, a reconciliation of payroll in the general ledger to quarterly 941s. Why? The company has an incentive to accurately file 941s since the returns are subject to audit by governmental authorities. If the 941s are correct, the reconciliation provides support for recorded payroll.

Additionally, consider the possibility of theft, such as duplicate payments or ghost employees. In a duplicate payment fraud, the thief, usually a payroll department employee, pays himself (or a friend) twice. Ghost employees exist when payroll personnel leave a terminated employee on the payroll. Why would someone in the payroll department intentionally leave a terminated employee in the payroll system? To steal the second payment. How? By changing the terminated employee's direct deposit bank account number to his own. The result? He receives two payments—his own and that of the terminated employee.

Retirement plans create additional risks of material misstatement. I often assess the classification, accuracy, and completeness assertions at high for such plans. Defined benefit and other postretirement plan accounting requirements are complex. Since the related accounting is difficult, errors can occur. Additionally, the related disclosures are challenging, and the accounting staff may not understand these requirements.

Substantive Procedures for Payroll

And finally, it's time to determine your substantive procedures in light of your identified risks.

My customary tests for auditing payroll are as follows:

- Reconcile quarterly 941s to payroll in the general ledger
- Analytically review salary expenses (see below)
- Recompute accrued payroll liability (amount recorded at period-end)
- Review payroll withholding accounts for appropriateness and vouch subsequent payments for any significant amounts
- Compare payroll expenses (including benefits) to budget or prior year balances and examine any unexplained variances
- When control weaknesses are present, design and perform procedures to address the related risks
- Compare accrued vacation to prior periods and current payroll activity
- Test pension and postretirement benefits for appropriate accounting, including disclosures

Analytical reviews of payroll could include comparing department salary expenses to total expenses and comparing the result to prior years.

Most entities do not have defined benefit plans or other postretirement benefits. But when such benefits are present, you will perform additional audit procedures such as testing census data, reconciling information to actuarial reports, obtaining benefit plan audit reports, testing assumptions, and recomputing benefits. Also, use a current disclosure checklist to vet the related disclosures. (Potential benefit plan types are numerous, so I am providing general audit ideas.)

Payroll controls can be tested for effectiveness. If the controls are effective, then some substantive procedures may not be necessary.

In light of my risk assessment and substantive procedures, what payroll work papers do I normally include in my audit files?

Common Payroll Work Papers

My payroll work papers normally include the following:

- An understanding of payroll-related internal controls
- Risk assessment of payroll at the assertion level
- Documentation of any payroll control deficiencies
- Payroll audit program
- Accrued salaries detail at period-end
- A summary of any significant payroll withholding accounts with supporting information
- A detail of vacation payable (if material) with comparisons to prior periods
- A comparison of current period payroll expenses with prior period expenses
- Budget to actual payroll reports
- A reconciliation of payroll in the general ledger to quarterly 941s
- Fraud-related payroll work papers when needed
- Disclosure checklist
- When pension or other postretirement benefits are present, related information such as tests of census information, tests of assumptions, plan documents, and actuarial reports

Auditing Payroll - A Simple Summary

- Primary relevant payroll assertions include completeness and cutoff for accrued payroll liabilities, occurrence for payroll expenses, and completeness, accuracy, and classification for retirement plan benefits
- Perform a walkthrough of the payroll cycle by making inquiries, inspecting documents, and making observations
- The directional risk for payroll is that it is understated
- Primary risks for payroll include:
  - Payroll is intentionally understated
  - Inappropriate parties receive payments
  - Employees receive duplicate payments
  - Employees receive inflated payments
  - Pensions and other post-employment benefits are improperly recorded or disclosed
- The substantive procedures for payroll should be responsive to the identified risks. Common procedures include:
  - Reconciling 941s to payroll
  - Recomputing accrued payroll liability
  - Reviewing payroll withholding accounts for appropriateness and vouching subsequent payments for any significant amounts
  - Comparing payroll expenses (including benefits) to budget or prior year balances and examining any unexplained variances
  - When control weaknesses are present, designing and performing procedures to address the related risks
  - Comparing accrued vacation to prior periods and current payroll activity
  - Testing pension and other postretirement expenses, related balance sheet accounts, and disclosures

Now you know how to audit payroll. Next we'll turn our attention to the audit of debt.

CHAPTER 11

The Why and How of Auditing Debt

What are the keys to auditing debt?

While auditing debt can be simple, sometimes it's tricky. For instance, classification issues can arise when debt covenant violations occur. Should the debt be classified as current or noncurrent? Likewise, some forms of debt (with detachable warrants) have equity characteristics, again leading to classification issues. Is it debt or equity—or both? Additionally, leases can create debt, even if that is not the intent.

Most of the time, however, auditing debt is simple. A company borrows money. An amortization schedule is created. And thereafter, debt service payments are made and recorded.

Either way, whether the process is complicated or simple, below I show you how to audit debt.

Auditing Debt — An Overview

In many governments, nonprofits, and small businesses, debt is a significant portion of total liabilities. Consequently, it is often a significant transaction area.

In this chapter, we will cover the following:

- Primary debt assertions
- Debt walkthroughs
- Directional risk for debt
- Primary risks for debt

- Common debt control deficiencies
- Risk of material misstatement for debt
- Substantive procedures for debt
- Common debt work papers

Primary Debt Assertions

First, let's look at assertions. The primary relevant debt assertions include completeness, classification, and obligation.

I believe, in general, completeness and classification are the most important debt assertions. When a company shows debt on its balance sheet, it is asserting that it is complete and classified correctly. By classification, I mean it is properly displayed as either short-term or long-term. I also mean the instrument is debt and recorded as such (and not equity). In regard to the obligation assertion, the company is asserting that the debt is owed by the company and not another entity.

Debt Walkthroughs

Second, perform your risk assessment work in light of the potential relevant assertions.

As you perform your debt walkthrough, ask questions or perform actions such as the following:

- Are there any debt covenant violations?
- If the company has violations, is the debt classified appropriately (usually current)?
- Is someone reconciling the debt in the general ledger to a loan amortization schedule?
- Inspect amortization schedules.
- Does the company have any unused lines of credit or other credit available?
- Inspect loan documents.

- Has the company refinanced its debt with another institution? Why?
- Who approves the borrowing of new money?
- Who approves new leases? Who handles lease accounting and are they competent?
- Does the company have any leases that should be recorded as debt?
- Inspect new loan and lease approvals.
- How are debt service payments made (e.g., by check or wire)? Who makes those payments?
- Are there any sinking funds? If yes, who is responsible for making deposits and payments?
- Observe the segregation of duties for persons:
  - Approving new loans
  - Receipting loan proceeds
  - Recording debt in the general ledger
  - Reconciling the debt in the general ledger to the loan amortization schedules
- Is the company required to file periodic reports with the lender? Inspect sample debt-related reports, if applicable.
- Does the company have any convertible debt or debt with detachable warrants? Are they properly recorded?
- Is the company following reporting framework requirements (e.g., FASB Codification) for debt?
- Is collateral pledged? If yes, what?
- What are the terms of the debt agreements?
- Is all debt recorded in the general ledger?
- Are debt issuance costs accounted for properly?
- Has the company guaranteed the debt of another entity?
- Are there standby letters of credit?

If control weaknesses exist, create audit procedures to address them. For example, if—during the walkthrough—we see that one person approves loans, deposits loan proceeds, and records the related debt, then we will perform fraud-related substantive procedures.

A company can fraudulently inflate its equity by intentionally omitting debt from its balance sheet. (Total assets equal liabilities plus equity. Therefore, if debt decreases, equity increases.)

As we saw with Enron, some entities place their debt on another company's balance sheet. (Enron did so using special purpose entities.) So, auditors need to consider that companies can intentionally omit debt from their balance sheets.

Another potential fraudulent presentation is showing short-term debt as long-term. When might this happen? When debt covenant violations occur. Such violations can trigger a requirement to reclassify long-term debt to short-term. If accounting personnel are aware of the requirement to classify debt as current and don't do so, then the reporting could be considered fraudulent.

Additionally, mistakes can lead to errors in debt accounting. Errors in accounting for debt can occur when principal payments are misclassified as expenses rather than debt reduction. Also, debt can erroneously be presented as long-term when it is current. Why? Maybe the company's accountant is not aware of the accounting rules. Also, some forms of debt, such as leases, can be difficult to interpret. Consequently, a company might errantly fail to record debt when required.

Directional Risk for Debt

Third, consider the directional risk of debt.

The directional risk for debt is that it is understated. Thus, make sure you audit for completeness and determine that all debt is recorded.

Primary Risks for Debt

Fourth, think about the risk related to debt. Primary risks for debt include:

- Debt is intentionally understated or omitted
- Debt is shown as noncurrent (due *more than* one year from the balance sheet date) though the amount is due *within* one year of the balance sheet date
- Leases are not recorded as debt though the reporting framework requires such accounting

It's obvious why a company might want to understate its debt. The company looks healthier. But why would a business desire to classify current debt as noncurrent? For the same reason: to make the company look stronger. By recording current debt as noncurrent, the company's working capital ratio (current assets divided by current liabilities) improves.

Common Debt Control Deficiencies

Fifth, think about control deficiencies noted during your walkthroughs and other risk assessment procedures.

In smaller entities, it is common to have the following control deficiencies:

- One person performs two or more of the following:
  - Approves new loans
  - Has the ability to borrow funds
  - Enters new debt in the accounting system
  - Deposits funds from the debt issuance
- Funds are borrowed without appropriate approval
- Debt postings are not agreed to amortization schedules
- Accounting personnel don't understand the accounting standards for debt (including lease accounting)

Risk of Material Misstatement for Debt

Sixth, assess your risk of material misstatement in light of the information you've gathered.

In auditing debt, the assertions that concern me the most are completeness, classification, and obligation. So the risk of material misstatement for these assertions is usually moderate to high.

My response to the higher risk assessments is to perform certain substantive procedures: namely, a review of debt covenant compliance and a review of debt and lease agreements—and the related accounting. Why?

As we saw above, debt covenant violations may require the company to reclassify debt from noncurrent to current. Doing so can be significant. The loan could be called by the lender, depending on the loan agreement. Proper classification of debt is critical.

Also, some leases should be recorded as debt. If such leases are not recorded, the company looks healthier than it is. Our audits should include procedures that address the completeness of debt and the obligations of the company.

Substantive Procedures for Debt

And finally, it's time to determine your substantive procedures in light of your identified risks.

My customary tests for auditing debt are as follows:

- Summarize and test debt covenants
- Review new leases to determine if debt should be recorded
- Confirm all significant debt with lenders
- Determine if all debt is classified appropriately (as current or noncurrent)
- Agree the end-of-period balances in the general ledger to the amortization schedules

- Agree future debt service payment summaries to amortization schedules
- Review accruals of any significant interest
- Review interest expense (usually comparing current and prior year)

I don't normally test controls related to debt. If controls are tested and you determine they are effective, then some of the substantive procedures listed above may not be necessary.

Common Debt Work Papers

My debt work papers normally include the following:

- An understanding of debt-related internal controls
- Documentation of any internal control deficiencies related to debt
- Risk assessment of debt at the assertion level
- Debt audit program
- A copy of all significant debt agreements (including lease and line-of-credit agreements)
- Minutes reflecting the approval of new debt
- A summary of debt activity (beginning balance plus new debt minus principal payments and ending balance)
- Amortization schedules for each debt
- Summary of all debt information for disclosure purposes (e.g., future debt service to be paid, interest rates, types of debt, collateral, etc.)
- Disclosure checklist

If there are questions regarding debt agreements and their presentation, I include additional language in the representation letter to address the issues. For example, if an owner loans funds to the company but there is no written debt agreement, the owner or management might verbally explain the arrangement. In such cases, I include language in the management representation letter to address the verbal assertions.

Auditing Debt - A Simple Summary

- Primary relevant debt assertions include completeness, classification, and obligation
- Perform a walkthrough of the debt cycle by making inquiries, inspecting documents, and making observations
- The directional risk for debt is that it is understated
- Primary risks for debt include:
  - Debt is intentionally understated or omitted
  - Debt is classified as noncurrent though it is current
  - Leases are not recorded as debt though the reporting framework requires such accounting
- The substantive procedures for debt should be responsive to the identified risks. Common procedures include:
  - Summarizing and testing debt covenants
  - Reviewing new leases to determine if debt should be recorded
  - Confirming all significant debt with lenders
  - Determining if all debt is classified appropriately (as current or noncurrent)
  - Agreeing the end-of-period debt balances in the general ledger to the amortization schedules
  - Agreeing future debt service payment summaries to amortization schedules
  - Reviewing accruals of any significant interest
  - Reviewing interest expense (usually comparing current and prior year)

Now you know how to audit debt. Next we'll turn our attention to the audit of equity.

CHAPTER 12

The Why and How of Auditing Equity

———

Auditing equity is easy, until it's not. Auditing equity is usually one of the easiest parts of an audit. For some equity accounts, you agree the year-end balances to the prior year ending balance, and you're done. For instance paid-in-capital seldom changes. Often, the only changes in equity are from current year profits and owner distributions. And testing those equity additions and reductions in equity usually takes just minutes.

Nevertheless, auditing equity can be challenging, especially for businesses that desire to attract investors. Such companies offer complicated equity instruments. Why? The desire to attract cash without giving away (too much) power. This balancing act can lead to complex equity instruments.

Regardless of whether a company's equity is easy to audit or not, below I show you how to focus on important equity issues.

Auditing Equity — An Overview

In this chapter, we will cover the following:

- Primary equity assertions
- Equity walkthroughs
- Directional risk for equity
- Primary risks for equity
- Common equity control deficiencies
- Risk of material misstatement for equity

- Substantive procedures for equity
- Common equity work papers

Primary Equity Assertions

First, let's look at assertions. Consider that equity comes in a variety of forms including:

- Common stock
- Paid-in-capital
- Preferred stock
- Treasury stock
- Accumulated other comprehensive income
- Noncontrolling interests
- Members' equity (for an LLC)
- Net assets (for a nonprofit)
- Net position (for a government)

Certain types of equity accounts are used for certain types of entities. For example, you'll find common stock in an incorporated business, net assets in nonprofits, and members' equity in a limited liability corporation.

The equity accounts used depend upon the type of entity and what occurs within and outside the organization. Examples include:

- Has an incorporated company purchased treasury stock?
- Does a nonprofit organization have donor-restricted contributions?
- Does a government have restricted net position?

It's a must that you understand the equity accounting requirements before you determine the relevant assertions.

Primary relevant equity assertions include:

- Existence and occurrence
- Rights and obligations
- Classification

When a company reflects equity on its balance sheet, it is asserting that the balance exists and that the equity transactions occurred. For example, if common stock is sold, the balance of the account is based upon the actual sale of stock and the monies received. In other words, the balance is properly recorded.

Equity instruments also have certain rights and obligations. For example, common stock provides rights to retained earnings. Some classes of stock provide voting privileges. Others do not.

Additionally, the classification of equity balances is important. Determining how to present equity is usually easy, but classification issues arise when an entity has convertible debt—is it debt or equity? Noncontrolling interests can also create questions about classification.

Equity Walkthroughs

Second, perform your risk assessment work in light of the potential relevant assertions. Early in your audit, perform a walkthrough of equity to see if there are any control weaknesses.

Here are sample questions and steps to use in your walkthrough:

- What types of equity does the entity have? What are the rights of each class?
- How many shares are authorized? How many shares are issued?
- Does the company have convertible debt?
- Has the company declared and paid dividends?
- Does the company have accumulated other comprehensive income?

- Inspect ownership documents such as stock certificates.
- Read the minutes to determine if any new equity was issued or if there were any buy-backs of stock.
- Is the entity attempting to raise additional capital?
- Is there a noncontrolling interest in the company?
- Does the company have a stock compensation plan?
- For a nonprofit, are there any restricted donations?
- For a government, is the net position restricted?
- For a limited liability corporation, are there differing classes of ownership?

As you ask the above questions, consider examining equity-related information such as stock certificates, cash receipts from new equity issuances, general ledger accounts, related journal entries, minutes, and stock compensation plan documents. Don't just ask questions. Observe equity controls and inspect sample documents such as stock certificates.

As you perform walkthroughs, also consider if there are risks of material misstatement due to fraud or error.

Directional Risk for Equity

Third, consider the directional risk of equity.

The directional risk for equity is that it is overstated since companies desire strong equity positions. Thus, make sure you audit for existence.

Primary Risks for Equity

Fourth, think about the risks related to equity. Primary risks for equity include:

- Equity is intentionally overstated
- Equity is misclassified
- Errors in equity accounting

Common Equity Control Deficiencies

Fifth, think about control deficiencies noted during your walkthroughs and other risk assessment work.

In smaller entities, it is common to have the following control deficiencies:

- One person performs two or more of the following:
  - Approves the sale of equity interests,
  - Records the new equity in the accounting system,
  - Deposits funds from the sale of equity instruments
- Accounting personnel lack sufficient knowledge regarding equity transactions and the requirements of the reporting framework (e.g., FASB)

Risk of Material Misstatement for Equity

Sixth, assess your risk of material misstatement in light of the information you've gathered. In most audit engagements, I assess control risk at high for each equity assertion.

In auditing equity, the assertions that concern me the most are existence and occurrence, rights and obligations, and classification. So, my inherent risk for these assertions is usually moderate to high.

My response to the higher risk assessments is to perform certain substantive procedures: namely, a review of equity transactions. Why? A company may desire to overstate its equity. Also, misclassifications or errors occur due to misunderstandings about equity accounting.

Substantive Procedures for Equity

And finally, it's time to determine your substantive procedures in light of your identified risks.

My normal substantive tests for auditing equity include:

- Summarizing and reviewing all equity transactions
- Reviewing all equity accounts for proper classification
- Agreeing all beginning-of-period balances to the prior period's ending balances
- Reviewing equity disclosures for compliance with the reporting framework requirements (e.g., GAAP)

I don't normally test controls related to equity. If controls are tested and you determine they are effective, then some of the substantive procedures may not be necessary.

In light of my risk assessment and substantive procedures, what equity work papers do I normally include in my audit files?

Common Equity Work Papers

My equity work papers normally include the following:

- An understanding of equity-related internal controls
- Documentation of internal control deficiencies related to equity
- Risk assessment of equity at the assertion level
- Equity audit program
- A copy of equity instruments
- Minutes reflecting the approval of new equity or the retirement of existing equity
- A summary of equity activity (beginning balances plus new equity less equity reductions and ending balance)
- Disclosure checklist

Auditing Equity – A Simple Summary

- Primary relevant equity assertions include existence and occurrence, rights and obligations, and classification
- Perform a walkthrough of equity by making inquiries, inspecting documents, and making observations

- The directional risk for equity is that it is overstated
- Primary risks for equity include:
  - Equity is intentionally overstated
  - Equity if misclassified
  - Errors in equity accounting
- The substantive procedures for equity should be responsive to the identified risks. Common procedures include:
  - Summarizing and reviewing all equity transactions
  - Reviewing all equity accounts for proper classification
  - Agreeing all beginning-of-period balances to the prior period's ending balances
  - Reviewing equity disclosures for compliance with the reporting framework requirements (e.g., GAAP)

Now you know how to audit equity.

We've completed our journey through the transaction areas. It's time to shift gears and wrap up the audit.

PART THREE

Wrapping Up the Audit

CHAPTER 13
The Why and How of Wrapping Up Audits

Do you ever have the *almost-done* illusion? You think you're almost done, but you're not—and you're not even close. Frustrating! Completing audits is not easy, but in this chapter, you'll learn how to cross the finish line with applause.

What? I'm Not Done?

I remember my boss asking me, "What's the status of the audit?" I answered, "Oh, I'm about 90% done." But I was actually at 75%—maybe. Why the miscalculation? I mistakenly thought if the planning and transaction areas (e.g., cash) were complete, I was nearly done. But I was wrong. Wrap-up takes (or least can take) a significant amount of time.

Wrapping Up Audits — An Overview

In the final stages of an audit, we are (among other things):

- Updating subsequent events
- Considering going concern
- Creating final analytics
- Providing audit entries to the client
- Summarizing passed journal entries
- Reviewing the file
- Creating financial statements
- Completing the disclosure checklist
- Documenting the close process
- Reviewing financial statements

- Obtaining a management representation letter
- Creating the audit opinion
- Creating a management letter
- Communicating control deficiencies

There is no required order for these steps. The sequence provided below is simply my normal process.

Let's start with subsequent events.

Updating Subsequent Events

The financial statements should disclose material subsequent events such as legal settlements, the issuance of debt, the adoption of a benefit plan, or the sale of stock. And while disclosure is important, subsequent events—such as legal settlements—can affect the year-end balance sheet. Some subsequent events trigger the accrual of liabilities.

Here are common subsequent event procedures:

- Inquire of management and the company attorneys about subsequent events
- Review the subsequent receipts and payments
- Read the minutes created after period-end
- Review the subsequent interim financial statements
- Review the subsequent year's budget
- Understand management's methods for accumulating subsequent event information

In performing these procedures, obtain subsequent event information through the audit report date.

If you've sent attorneys' letters asking about potential litigation, you may need to get an update to coincide with the audit report date. You want the attorney's written response to be as close to the audit report date as possible. How close? Usually within two weeks. If there are significant issues, you may need to bring the written response through the audit report date.

Another critical issue during wrap-up is going concern.

Considering Going Concern

Even in the planning stage, auditors should consider going concern, especially if the entity is struggling financially. But as you approach the end of the audit, going concern should crystallize. Now you have your audit evidence, and it's time to determine if a going concern opinion is necessary. Also, consider whether going concern disclosures are sufficient. If substantial doubt is present, then the entity should include going concern disclosures even if substantial doubt is alleviated by management's plans.

And what is substantial doubt? The Financial Accounting Standards Board defines it this way:

> *Substantial doubt* about the entity's ability to continue as a going concern is considered to exist when aggregate conditions and events indicate that it is *probable* that the entity will be unable to meet obligations when due within one year of the date that the financial statements are issued or are available to be issued.

So, for nongovernmental entities, ask "Is it probable that the company will meet its obligations for one year from the opinion date?" If it is probable that the entity will meet its obligations, then substantial doubt does not exist. If it is *not* probable that the entity will meet its obligations, then substantial doubt exists.

And what is the period of time to be considered when assessing going concern? One year from the audit report date—unless the entity is a government. If the entity is a government, then the evaluation period is one year from the financial statement date though this period can lengthen in certain circumstances.

The going concern evaluation is one that *management* makes as it considers whether disclosures are necessary.

Then the *auditor* considers going concern from an audit perspective. If substantial doubt is present and is not alleviated, the auditor issues a going concern opinion. Also, if going concern disclosures are incorrect or inadequate, the auditor may need to modify the opinion.

Wrap-up also includes the creation and review of final analytics.

Creating Final Analytics

Auditors create *planning* analytics—the comparison of key numbers—early in the audit. Why? To look for the risk of material misstatement. Unexpected changes in numbers are indicators of potential error or fraud. They create questions. When unexpected variations exist, auditors plan procedures to see why. (See Appendix A for a detailed look at planning analytics.)

What is the purpose of *final* analytics? To determine whether unanswered questions still exit. Auditors want to know, given the audit evidence in hand, that the numbers are fairly stated.

What final analytics should you use? Audit standards don't specify particular analytics. Some auditors read the financial statements (when comparative periods are presented). Others review key ratios. And some compare current year trial balance numbers with the prior year.

My final analytics are often the same as those in the beginning. For example, if my planning analytics include a comparison of trial balance numbers, so will my final analytics. Why do I use the same analytics? I want to know that the questions raised in the beginning are now answered.

Next, you are ready to provide your proposed audit entries.

Providing Audit Entries to the Client

Give your audit entries to your client. Hopefully, you discussed these adjustments with your client when you discovered them. If you did, this part is easy. You're just giving your client the entries. If not, review the proposed adjustments with the client and see if they agree.

Your client may desire to omit recording some immaterial entries, and that's okay as long as they are not material.

Summarizing Passed Journal Entries

Prior to creating the representation letter, the auditor needs to summarize passed journal entries. Why? Audit standards require management to provide a written assertion regarding whether the uncorrected misstatements are immaterial. The summary assists in that determination.

Once you summarize the uncorrected misstatements, you should consider whether they are material. Review your audit materiality and determine whether the passed adjustments are acceptable. If material uncorrected misstatements exist, consider the effect on your opinion.

In addition to the above, you need to review the audit file to make sure everything is in order.

Reviewing the File

Perform your final review of the work papers and sign off as the reviewer. All preparer and reviewer dates must precede or coincide with the representation letter date (which is the opinion date). Why? Reviews are a part of your evidential matter. Documentation—including reviews—must exist no later than the opinion date.

Once the audit file is ready, it's time to create the financial statements, if you've been engaged to do so.

Creating Financial Statements

Larger entities usually create their own financial statements, but smaller organizations sometimes outsource this work to their auditors.

If the auditor creates the financial statements, the following needs to occur:

- The audit firm creates the financial statements
- The audit firm reviews the financial statements
- The client reviews the financial statements

If you (the auditor) are engaged to create the financial statements, complete them on time. Why? Management must read and take responsibility for the financial statements prior to signing the representation letter.

Also, the auditor's review of the financial statements needs to be completed prior to the date of management's representation letter. Why? All evidential matter, including the audit firm's review of the financial statements, must be complete before the opinion is issued.

Management *and* the auditor must review the financial statements before the opinion is issued. We'll discuss the auditor's financial statement review process in a moment, but before we do, let's take a look at completing the disclosure checklist.

Completing the Disclosure Checklist

Whether you or your client creates the financial statements, a disclosure checklist helps ensure the completeness and propriety of the notes. Remember your audit opinion covers the financial statements and the disclosures.

Since new accounting standards are issued throughout the year, make sure you use a current disclosure checklist. Otherwise, you may not be aware of new or amended disclosure requirements.

Documenting the Close Process

Regardless of who prepares the financial statements, the auditor should agree the financial statements to the underlying accounting records. Additionally, you should review any journal entries used to create the financial statements. These steps should be documented in the audit file.

Now it's time to review the financial statements.

Reviewing Financial Statements

If your audit firm creates the financial statements, at least two people should be involved—one creating and one reviewing. Why? Two reasons: (1) the self-review threat (an independence issue) and (2) blind spots.

What is a self-review threat? It's the idea that the person creating something (e.g., the financial statements) will not be independent in reviewing the same. Why is this a problem? Well, we are issuing an *independent* auditor's opinion. That's why we need a second-person review of the financial statements—to mitigate the self-review threat.

Additionally, a second-person review uncovers blind spots. If I create financial statements with errors, I may not see my own mistakes. I have blind spots. Such errors are often readily apparent to a second person.

Once the financial statements have been prepared and reviewed by your audit firm and your client, it's time to obtain the management representation letter.

Obtaining a Management Representation Letter

The management representation letter is usually prepared by the audit firm and is provided to the client for signing. The letter addresses issues and information such as:

- Management's responsibility for the financial statements
- Management's responsibility for internal controls
- Assurances that all transactions have been recorded
- Whether fraud occurred
- Whether non-compliance with laws or regulations occurred
- The effects of uncorrected misstatements
- Whether litigation exists or is threatened
- The assumptions used in computing estimates
- Related party transactions
- Subsequent events
- Supplementary information
- Responsibility for nonattest services

The representation letter should cover all financial statements and periods referred to in the auditor's report. If management refuses to provide the management letter, then consider the effect upon the auditor's report. Such a refusal constitutes a scope limitation and will usually preclude the issuance of an unmodified opinion.

Another part of wrap-up is creating your audit opinion.

Creating the Audit Opinion

You've planned and performed your audit. Now you need to consider the type of opinion to issue. If an unmodified opinion is merited, no problem. Issue a standard opinion. But if you qualify the opinion, or issue a disclaimer or an adverse opinion, there's more work to be done.

Determine which opinion is appropriate. Most CPAs use sample reports from national publishing companies. Others use sample reports directly from the auditing standards. Regardless, place a copy of the sample report in your audit file. Why? Your peer reviewer—or someone else—might question your report language. Responding to such questions is much easier with the sample report in hand.

Create your opinion and have a second person review the report, comparing the opinion to the sample report. Check and recheck your wording.

Another consideration in wrap-up is whether you'll issue a management letter.

Creating a Management Letter

While not required, you can provide a written management letter to your audit client. Why would you do so? To add value to the audit. What is a management letter? Suggestions from the auditor to improve the business.

What should you include in the letter? It's up to you (and dependent upon your observations during the audit), but here are a few examples:

- Suggested monthly reports for the owners or management
- Warnings regarding cyber attacks and prevention techniques
- A suggestion that excess cash be used to pay off high interest rate debt
- Procurement and bidding recommendations
- A suggestion that security cameras be installed
- Software recommendations
- A suggestion that the company review its property insurance coverage
- Best practices for implementing new accounting standards

If you provide a management letter, give the client a draft prior to issuance. Why? To avoid the embarrassment of making inappropriate suggestions—maybe they've already done what you are suggesting.

In addition to the management letter, you may need to communicate significant deficiencies and material weaknesses.

Communicating Control Deficiencies

Audit standards define significant deficiencies and material weaknesses as follows:

- Significant deficiency. A deficiency, or a combination of deficiencies, in internal control that is less severe than a material weakness yet important enough to merit attention by those charged with governance.
- Material weakness. A deficiency, or a combination of deficiencies, in internal control, such that there is a reasonable possibility that a material misstatement of the entity's financial statements will not be prevented, or detected and corrected, on a timely basis.

Auditing standards require a written communication of significant deficiencies and material weaknesses.

Control deficiencies are often noted during the risk assessment process, particularly as you perform walkthroughs.

You may also note control weaknesses as you prepare audit journal entries, especially if the adjustments are material. Misstatements are often the result of weak internal controls.

Regardless of how you become aware of the control weaknesses, capture them immediately. Otherwise, you may forget them later. Also, if control weaknesses are important, you may need to communicate them to management *when* they are discovered, and do so again at the completion of the audit.

During wrap-up, create your internal control letter based on the weaknesses noted during the audit.

Consider providing a draft of the internal control letter to management prior to final issuance. Why? To avoid potential misunderstandings. If there's a disagreement between the client and the auditor, it's best to discuss the issue prior to final issuance of the internal control letter.

One other suggestion: if there are sensitive issues, the senior audit team member (usually the engagement partner) should make this communication. It's time to speak the truth with tactfulness—and experience helps.

I started this chapter by saying that wrap-up can take a significant amount of time. As we have seen, there is much to be done in the closing stage of the engagement.

Wrapping Up Audits - A Simple Summary

- Perform subsequent event procedures to ensure that all relevant information is included in the financial statements
- Consider whether going concern disclosures are necessary and, if required, complete; also consider the need for a going concern opinion
- Create final analytics and determine if all significant variations in the numbers have been addressed
- Provide proposed audit entries to the client
- Summarize and review all passed journal entries to ensure that material misstatements are not present
- Review the work paper file
- Create the financial statements (if you have been engaged to do so)
- Complete a current disclosure checklist
- Agree the financial statements to the client's underlying information
- Review the financial statements
- Obtain a signed management representation letter

- Create the audit opinion
- Create a management letter
- Communicate significant deficiencies and material weaknesses

There you have it: the wrap-up process. Now, when your boss asks, "What's the status of the audit?", you can say, "I'm at 90 percent"— and be sure of it.

CONCLUSION

Let the wise hear and increase in learning.
Proverbs 1:5

In the preface I said, "When you're done with this book, you'll understand auditing, possibly in a way you never have. Then you'll audit with greater confidence." Now that you've made the journey, I hope your confidence is higher and your knowledge is greater. But as we close the book, let's go beyond knowledge and consider wisdom.

When I graduated from college in 1984, I thought I was ready to conquer the audit world. Thirty-five years later, I realize how little I knew. Along the way, I've struggled, made (many) mistakes, and grown. That's life, is it not? So, apply the concepts in this book and learn, knowing that auditing is more art than science, more wisdom than knowledge.

I leave you with a story.

My Story

I said to my wife, "Am I driving straight?" I felt as if I was weaving, not quite in control. I felt dizzy and I could hear clicking noises in my ear.

The mystery increased over the next two years as I visited three different doctors. They stuck, prodded, and probed me, but no solution.

Frustrating.

Meanwhile, I felt a growing numbness on the right side of my face. So one night I started Googling health websites (the thing they tell you not to do) and came upon this link: *Acoustic Neuroma Association*. I clicked it. As I read the symptoms, it was like reading my diary. It couldn't be. A brain tumor.

The next day I handed my doctor the acoustic neuroma information and said, "I think this is what I have. I want a brain scan."

Two days later, while on the golf course, I received the doctor's call. "Mr. Hall, you were right. You have a 2.3-centimeter brain tumor." (I sent him a bill for my diagnosis but never got paid—just kidding.) My golfing buddies gathered around and prayed for me on the 17th green, and I went home to break the news to my wife. At the time, I had two children, two and five. I was deeply concerned, but at peace nonetheless.

Shortly afterwards, I was in a surgeon's office in Atlanta. The doctor said they'd do a ten-hour operation. There was a 40% chance of paralysis and a 5% chance of death. The tumor was too large for radiation—or so I was told.

I didn't like the odds, so I prayed more and went back to the Internet. There I (providentially) found Dr. Jeffrey Williams at Johns Hopkins Hospital in Baltimore. I emailed the good doctor, telling him of the tumor's size. His response was, "I radiate tumors that size every day." He was a pioneer in fractionated stereotactic radiation, one of the few physicians in the world using this technique at the time.

A few days later, I'm lying on an operating table in Baltimore with my head bolted down, ready for radiation. They bolt you down to ensure the cooking of the tumor (and not the brain). Fun, you should try it. Four more times I visited the table. Each time everyone left the room, a sure sign you should not do this at home.

Each day I laid there silently, talking to God and trusting in Him.

Three weeks later I returned to work. Turn the clock forward twenty years and I have had two sick days. No paralysis. I am mostly deaf in my right ear, but no complaints. I'm still here!

I watched my children grow up. Baseball games, piano recitals, hikes in the woods, Christmas mornings, Easter mornings, vacations in the Smokeys, graduations. My children are now twenty-two and twenty-five. My wife is still at my side, and I'm thankful.

So what does a brain tumor story teach us about audits? (You might, at this point, be thinking: they *did* cook the wrong part.)

Audit Lessons from a Brain Tumor

1. Pay Attention to Signs

It's easy to overlook the obvious. Maybe we don't want to see a red flag. (I didn't *want* to believe I had a tumor.) It might slow us down. But an audit is not purely about finishing and billing. It's about gathering proper evidential matter to support the opinion. To do less is delinquent and dangerous.

2. Seek Alternatives

If you can't gain appropriate audit evidence one way, seek another. Don't simply push forward, using the same procedures year after year. The doctor in Atlanta was a surgeon, so his solution was surgery. His answer was based on his tools, his normal procedures. If you've always used a hammer, try a wrench.

3. Seek Counsel

If one answer doesn't ring true, see what someone else says, maybe even someone outside your firm. Obviously, you need to make sure your engagement partner agrees about seeking outside guidance, but if he or she gives the green light, go for it. I often call the AICPA hotline. I find them helpful and knowledgeable. I also have relationships with other professionals, so I call friends and ask their opinions—and they call me. I check my pride at the door. I'd rather look dumb and be right than to look smart and be wrong.

4. Embrace Change

Fractionated stereotactic radiation was new. Dr. Williams was a pioneer in the technique. The only way your audit processes will get better is to try new techniques: paperless software (we use Caseware), data mining (we use IDEA), real fraud inquiries (I use Association of Certified Fraud Examiner techniques), electronic bank confirmations (we use Confirmation.com), project management software (I use Basecamp). If you are still pushing a pentel on a four-column, it's time to change.

Postscript

Finally, remember that work is important, but life itself is the best gift. Be thankful for each moment, each hour, each day.

Cheers!

APPENDICES

APPENDIX A
Preliminary Analytics

Auditors often struggle with creating and using preliminary analytics, so let's take a look at how to use this risk assessment tool.

Below, we'll cover the following:

- The purpose of planning analytics
- Gaining an understanding of the business
- Expectations and results
- The best types of planning analytics
- Documenting planning analytics
- Conclusion: no risk identified
- Conclusion: risk identified
- Linking to the audit plan
- Planning analytics for first-year businesses
- Planning analytics for fraudulent revenue recognition

The Purpose of Planning Analytics

The purpose of preliminary analytics (also called planning analytics) is to identify risks of material misstatement.

What are planning analytics? A review of comparative numbers and ratios. Why? To see if *unexpected changes* or *unusual relationships* are present.

Numbers have relationships. For example, if debt increases, interest expense should likewise increase, assuming interest rates are constant. Knowing what is normal allows us to see what is abnormal.

Other examples of normal relationships include:

- If sales increase, the cost of goods sold should increase
- If the number of employees decrease, payroll expense should decrease
- If an operating lease is unchanged, year-to-year rent expense should be about the same

Unexpected changes in numbers are risk indicators—specifically, risks of material misstatement. And when risks of material misstatement are present, responses (audit procedures) should follow. This is why we create planning analytics: to see if there are any risks that should be addressed with audit procedures.

Given that planning analytics are risk assessment procedures, when should we employ them?

Gaining an Understanding of the Business

Create your expectations and preliminary analytics *after* gaining an understanding of the entity. Why? Context determines reasonableness. It tells you what *normal* is.

Here are examples of what you need to know about the entity:

- Are there competitive pressures?
- What are the company's objectives?
- Are there cash flow problems?
- What are the normal profit margins for each product?
- Does the organization have debt?
- Who owns the company?
- Are there related parties?
- What are the current year operational results?
- Is the workforce higher, lower, or stable?
- Have the units sold increased, decreased, or remained stable?
- Are there any major construction projects?

Additionally, you can better understand what to expect by considering past changes in numbers. Reading the current year minutes and considering industry changes also provides context.

Once you know what to expect, you are ready to create your planning analytics.

Expectations and Results

Sometimes the numbers are as expected. If they are, then a risk of material misstatement is not present (at least, there is no indication of it). But in most audits, some unexpected changes or unusual relationships are present.

For example, what if you expect sales to decrease 10%, but they are up 15%? Then a red flag is waving. Or what if you expect sales to remain constant, but there is a 25% increase? Then fraud could be present. Such anomalies are risk indicators.

Once you develop your expectations, what types of analytics should you create?

The Best Types of Planning Analytics

Auditing standards don't specify the types of planning analytics to use. But some, in my opinion, are better than others. Here's my approach for most engagements.

First, I create my planning analytics at the financial statement reporting level. Why? Well, that's what the financial statement reader sees. The reader doesn't see, for example, the trial balance numbers. If financial statement level numbers are not available early in the audit, then I use the trial balance numbers. Also, if unexpected changes are noted in financial statement level analytics, I might add trial-balance-level comparisons. Why? To better understand the variations.

Regardless, perform *revenue* analytics at a more granular level.

Why? As we'll see below (in the section titled *Planning Analytics for Fraudulent Revenue Recognition*), detailed revenue analytics are called for by audit standards.

Second, add any key industry ratios monitored by management and those charged with governance. Often, auditors present these key numbers in their exit conference with the board, maybe in a slide presentation. If the ratios are important to the board at the end of the audit, then they are—or least they should be—important to the auditor at the beginning.

Examples of key industry ratios include:

- Inventory turnover
- Return on equity
- Days cash on hand
- Gross profit
- Debt/Equity

Okay, so we know what analytics to create, but how do we document them?

Documenting Planning Analytics

Here are my suggestions for documenting your planning analytics.

- Document overall expectations
- Document comparisons of prior-year / current-year numbers (you might include multiple prior year comparisons, if available)
- Document key industry ratio comparisons
- Summarize your conclusions, including whether risks were noted
- Place the identified risks on your summary risk assessment form

Your conclusions should state whether a risk of material misstatement was identified—or not.

Conclusion: No Risk Identified

What if, in the planning analytics, there are no unexpected changes? Then no identified risk is present.

Even so, you should document your conclusion. For example:

Conclusion: I reviewed the planning analytics and noted no unexpected changes. No risks of material misstatement were identified.

Conclusion: Risk Identified

Alternatively, you might see unexpected changes. You thought certain numbers would remain constant, but they moved significantly. Or you expected material changes, but none were present.

Again, document your conclusion. For example:

Conclusion: I expected payroll to remain constant since the company's workforce remained at approximately 425 employees. Payroll expenses increased, however, by 15% (almost $3.8 million). There is a risk of material misstatement in relation to payroll expenses.

Now, it's time to place the identified risks (if there are any) on your summary risk assessment form.

Linking to the Audit Plan

I summarize all risks of material misstatement on my summary risk assessment form. These risks might come from walkthroughs, planning analytics, or other risk assessment procedures. Regardless, I want them in one place.

The final step in the audit risk assessment process is to link your identified risks to your audit program. If there's a risk, there should be a response (an audit procedure).

Auditors often believe that planning analytics are not feasible for first-year businesses. But is this true? Not really.

Planning Analytics for First-Year Businesses

So, how can you create planning analytics for a new business?

Here are four options:

1. Use non-financial information

Compute expected numbers using non-financial information (e.g., number of widgets sold times price). Then compare the calculated numbers to the general ledger and look for unexpected variances.

2. Use ratios

Calculate ratios common to the entity's industry and compare the results to industry benchmarks.

While industry analytics can be computed, I'm not sure how useful they are for a new company. Infant companies do not normally generate numbers comparable to more mature entities. But we'll keep this choice in our quiver—just in case.

3. Use intra-period numbers

Compare intra-period numbers. Discuss the expected monthly or quarterly revenue trends with the client before you examine the accounting records. The warehouse foreman might say, "We shipped almost nothing the first six months. Then things caught fire. My head was spinning the last half of the year."

Does the general ledger reflect this story? Did revenues and costs of goods sold significantly increase in the latter half of the year?

4. Use budgetary numbers

Review budgetary comparisons. Some entities, such as governments, lend themselves to this alternative. Others (those without budgets) do not.

Finally, let's consider audit requirements in relation to fraudulent revenue recognition. Generally accepted auditing standards (in the United States) require analytics for revenue accounts.

Planning Analytics for Fraudulent Revenue Recognition

AU-C 240.22 says, "[T]he auditor should evaluate whether unusual or unexpected relationships that have been identified indicate risks of material misstatement due to fraud. To the extent not already included, the analytical procedures, and evaluation thereof, should include procedures relating to revenue accounts."

The auditing standards suggest a more detailed form of analytics for revenues. AU-C 240.A25 offers the following possibilities:

- A comparison of sales volume, as determined from recorded revenue amounts, with production capacity
- A trend analysis of revenues by month and sales returns by month, during and shortly after the reporting period
- A trend analysis of sales by month compared with units shipped

In light of these suggested procedures and the potential for fraud, it is prudent to create revenue analytics at a detailed level.

Preliminary Analytics - A Simple Summary

- Planning analytics are created for the purpose of identifying risks of material misstatement in the form of unexpected changes in numbers or unusual relationships
- Develop your expectations before creating your planning analytics
- Create analytics at the financial statement or trial balance level
- Compute key industry ratios

- Conclude about whether risks of material misstatement are present
- Summarize your risks of material misstatement on your summary risk assessment form
- Link your identified risks of material misstatement to your audit program
- Prepare planning analytics for first-year businesses using comparisons such as:
  - Non-financial information with financial results
  - Industry ratios with the company's ratios
  - Intra-period numbers (e.g., month-to-month)
  - Budget and actual numbers
- Audit standards require analytics for revenues (to look for fraud)

APPENDIX B
Understanding the Audit Risk Model

———

Remember the cowboy movie *The Good, The Bad, The Ugly*? Well, in audits we have the same.

The Good: the audit firm issues an unmodified opinion and the financial statements are fairly stated. Moreover, the audit file properly supports the opinion.

The Bad: the audit firm issues an unmodified opinion and the financial statements are fairly stated, but the work papers are weak. The audit firm just got lucky.

The Ugly: the audit firm issues an unmodified opinion but the financial statements are *not* fairly stated. Material error (or fraud) is present. And the audit file…well, we won't go there. It's ugly.

Audit failure occurs when an audit firm issues an unmodified opinion and the financial statements are not fairly stated. A material misstatement is present and the auditor doesn't know it.

Material misstatements occur and remain in financial statements when:

- Internal controls (a responsibility of the company) fail or are improperly designed
- Audit work (a responsibility of the auditor) is lacking

Auditing standards (AU-C 200.14) defines audit risk as "the risk that the auditor expresses an inappropriate audit opinion when the financial statements are materially misstated. Audit risk is a function of the risks of material misstatement and detection risk."

In other words, audit risk is the result of what the company does or does not do *and* what the auditor does or does not do.

Audit Risk Model

Audit risk is defined as:

Inherent risk X Control risk X Detection risk

I like to think of these three elements as follows:

- Inherent risk - the nature of the transaction or disclosure (risky or not risky)
- Control risk - the chance that material misstatements will not be prevented or detected by internal controls
- Detection risk - the chance that material misstatement will not be detected by the auditors

The first two (inherent risk and control risk) live in the company's accounting system; the third (detection risk) lies with the audit firm. The extent of the auditor's work should increase as the risk of material misstatement increases. Proper audit work decreases detection risk (the risk that the auditor will fail to detect material misstatements).

Inherent Risk

Some transactions are more likely to be misstated. They are *inherently risky.* Why? Reasons include:

- The complexity of the transaction (e.g., derivatives)
- The asset is easy to steal (e.g., cash)
- The need for judgment (e.g., a bank's allowance for loan losses)
- The volume of transactions is high (e.g., cash)
- The accounting personnel are inexperienced or lack sufficient knowledge

Inherent risk is what a transaction *is*, independent of related controls. Some transactions are more prone to misstatement. Others are not. And where does inherent risk come from? The transaction's nature or its environment.

Control Risk

Internal controls are necessary when a transaction is risky. Why? To monitor and manage the risk. Think about the words *internal control*. First, *internal* means the control occurs within the company. Second, *control* means to manage.

Since some transactions are more prone to theft or error, companies need internal controls to prevent or detect misstatements.

Examples of internal controls include:

- The reconciliation of monthly bank statements to the general ledger
- Receipting clerks are not allowed to reconcile bank statements (to enhance segregation of duties)
- The cash supervisor reviews the daily work of collections personnel
- A department head reviews and approves bi-weekly time records before payroll is processed
- The accounting supervisor reviews all new vendors added by the payable clerks to ensure legitimacy

If internal controls are designed appropriately and work correctly, the financial statements should be materially correct. But if the internal controls are absent or ineffective, material misstatements can occur. What then? Well, it's up to the auditor.

Detection Risk

The auditor is tasked with detecting material misstatements. If he or she does not, audit failure occurs. The audit firm issues an unmodified opinion but a material misstatement is present.

Auditors decrease detection risk—the risk that material misstatements will not be detected—by appropriately planning and performing their work.

Understanding the Audit Risk Model - A Simple Summary

- Audit failure occurs when an auditor issues an unmodified opinion and a material misstatement is present
- Audit Risk = Inherent risk X Control risk X Detection risk
- Inherent risk is the nature of the transaction or disclosure
- Control risk is the chance that material misstatements will not be prevented or detected by internal controls
- Detection risk is the chance that material misstatements will not be detected by the auditor
- Internal controls—if designed well and working correctly—prevent or detect material misstatements
- Audits—if designed well and performed correctly—detect material misstatements

APPENDIX C
Audit Documentation

———

Peer reviewers are saying, "If it's not documented, it's not done." Why? Because standards require sufficient audit documentation. And if audit work is not documented, the peer reviewer can't give credit.

But what does sufficient documentation mean? What should be in our work papers? How much is necessary? This appendix answers these questions.

In the AICPA's Enhanced Oversight Program, one in four audits is *nonconforming* due to a lack of sufficient documentation. This has been and continues to be a hot-button issue in peer reviews. And it's not going away.

Auditors ask, "What is sufficient documentation?" That's the problem, isn't it? The answer is not black and white. But we all know good documentation when we see it—and poor as well.

Poor Work Papers

Too often work papers are lacking. Why?

First, many times it boils down to profit. Auditors can make more money by doing less work. Let's state the obvious: quality documentation takes more time and may lessen profit. But what's the other choice? Poor work.

Second, the auditor may not understand the audit requirements.

In this case, it's not motive (more profit), it's a lack of understanding.

Third, another contributing factor is that firms bid for work—and low price usually carries the day. Then, when it's time to do the work, there's not enough budget (time)—and quality suffers. Corners are cut. Planning is disregarded. Audit programs are poorly designed. Confirmations, walkthroughs, fraud inquiries are omitted.

These three reasons may be true, but we all know that quality is the foundation of every good CPA firm. And work papers tell the story—the real story—about a firm's character.

How would you rate your quality? Is it excellent, average, poor? If you had to put your last audit file on a public website, would you be proud? Or does it need improvement?

To assist you in making that assessment, consider the differences in *insufficient* and *sufficient* audit documentation.

Insufficient Audit Documentation

First, let's look at examples of insufficient documentation:

- Signing off on audit steps with no supporting work papers (and no explanation on the audit program)
- Putting a client-prepared document in the audit file with no audit work performed
- Not signing off on audit steps
- Failing to reference audit steps to supporting work papers
- Listing a series of numbers in an Excel spreadsheet without indicating where they came from and who provided them
- Not signing off on work papers as a preparer
- Not signing off on work papers as the reviewer
- Failing to place excerpts of key documents in the file (e.g., debt agreement)

- Performing fraud inquiries but not documenting who was interviewed (their name) and when (the date)
- Not documenting the selection of a sample, like the sample size, the reason for the sample, and how it was taken
- Failing to provide the basis for low inherent risk assessments
- Not sending confirmations for key bank accounts and debt
- A failure to document the reason for not sending receivable confirmations
- A lack of retrospective reviews
- A failure to document the *current* year walkthroughs for significant transaction cycles
- Not documenting COSO control deficiencies (e.g., control environment, management's risk assessment procedures)
- A failure to document risk assessments
- Low control risk assessments without a test of controls
- A lack of linkage from the risk assessment to the audit plan
- No independence documentation though nonattest services are provided

While this list is not comprehensive, it provides examples. Probably the worst offense (at least in my mind) is signing off on an audit program step though the procedure was not performed.

Sufficient Audit Documentation

Now, let's examine what constitutes *sufficient* documentation.

AU-C 230 *Audit Documentation* defines how auditors are to create audit evidence. It says that an experienced auditor with no connection to the audit should understand the:

- Nature, timing, and extent of procedures performed
- Results and evidence obtained
- Significant findings, issues, and professional judgments

While most auditors are familiar with these requirements, the difficulty lies in making this happen.

Experienced Auditor's Understanding

Here's the key: When an experienced auditor reviews the documentation, does that person understand the work?

Any good communicator makes it his job to speak or write in an understandable way. In creating work papers, we are the communicators. The responsibility for transmitting the message lies with us, the work paper preparers.

A Lack of Clarity in Work Papers

Why do work papers lack clarity? The work paper preparer forgets he has an audience. As we prepare work papers, we need to think about those who will review them. All too often, the person creating a work paper understands what he is doing, but the reviewer does not. Why? The message is not clear.

Creating Clarity

To create clarity, include the following:

- A purpose statement
- The source of the information
- The identification of who prepared and reviewed the work paper
- The audit evidence
- A conclusion

When I make these suggestions, some auditors push back saying, "We've already documented some of this information in the audit program."

That may be true, but I am telling you—after reviewing thousands of audit files—the message (what is being done and why) can get lost. Reviewers often (speaking for myself) have a difficult time understanding how the work relates to the audit program—and the work paper's purpose.

Remember, the work paper preparer is responsible for communicating clearly.

And here's another thing to consider. You (the work paper preparer) might spend six hours on one document. You are keenly aware of what you did. But the reviewer, on the other hand, might have five minutes—and he is trying as quickly as possible to understand.

Help Your Reviewers

Communicate to work paper reviewers by:

1. Telling them what you are doing (provide a purpose statement)
2. Performing the work (clearly document what is done)
3. Telling them how it went (state the conclusion)

Firms may want to adopt a standard location (e.g., top left-hand corner of each work paper) for the purpose and conclusion statements. You may also want to highlight this wording with a certain color (e.g., blue) so it stands out. Such consistency adds clarity and speeds the review.

Too Much Audit Documentation

It's funny, but many CPAs say to me, "I feel like I do too much work," meaning they believe they are auditing more than is necessary. To which I respond, "I agree."

In reviewing audit files, I see:

- The clutter of unnecessary work papers
- Documents received from clients that don't support the audit opinion
- Unnecessary work performed on these extraneous documents

For whatever reason, audit clients provide unrequested documents. And then—for some other reason—we retain them, even if not needed.

If we add a purpose statement, we'll discover that *some* work papers are not needed. Great. Then we can get rid of them. As we remove clutter, communication becomes clearer. And your reviewers (the in-charge or partner) will thank you for it.

Audit Documentation - A Simple Summary

- If it's not documented, it's not done
- Poor work papers are often the result of taking too many shortcuts (or not performing the work at all)
- Work papers should provide the following in an understandable manner:
  - Nature, timing, and extent of procedures performed
  - Results and evidence obtained
  - Significant findings, issues, and professional judgments
- In preparing a work paper you are documenting and communicating your work
- The responsibility for clear communication lies with the work paper preparer
- Ask yourself, "Can an experienced auditor easily understand what was done?"
- Communicate more clearly by providing:
  - A purpose statement
  - What was done
  - A conclusion
  - The source of information
  - The preparer's name
  - Defined tickmarks
- Remove work papers that have no purpose

AUTHOR INFORMATION

Charles Hall is a Certified Public Accountant in the United States. He is also a Certified Fraud Examiner. He frequently speaks at continuing education events for CPAs and is a blogger at CPAHallTalk.com.

This is Charles' third book, the first being *The Little Book of Local Government Fraud Prevention* and the second, *Preparation of Financial Statements and Compilation Engagements*.

Charles is the quality control partner at McNair, McLemore, Middlebrooks & Co, LLC in Macon, Georgia. As such, he works with audit professionals on a daily basis. He has audited governments, nonprofits, and commercial entities since 1985.

Charles received his Master's Degree in Accounting from the University of Georgia in 1984.

Made in United States
North Haven, CT
14 December 2021

12786436R00087